RUNNING WITH EMUS

MERRILEE MOSS

CURRENCY PRESS
The performing arts publisher

CURRENCY PLAYS

First published in 2020
by Currency Press Pty Ltd,
PO Box 2287, Strawberry Hills, NSW, 2012, Australia
enquiries@currency.com.au
www.currency.com.au

in association with La Mama Theatre Company, Melbourne

Copyright: *Running with Emus* © Merrilee Moss, 2020.

COPYING FOR EDUCATIONAL PURPOSES

The Australian *Copyright Act 1968* (Act) allows a maximum of one chapter or 10% of this book, whichever is the greater, to be copied by any educational institution for its educational purposes provided that that educational institution (or the body that administers it) has given a remuneration notice to Copyright Agency (CA) under the Act.
For details of the CA licence for educational institutions contact CA, 11/66 Goulburn Street, Sydney, NSW, 2000; tel: within Australia 1800 066 844 toll free; outside Australia 61 2 9394 7600; fax: 61 2 9394 7601; email: info@copyright.com.au

COPYING FOR OTHER PURPOSES

Except as permitted under the Act, for example a fair dealing for the purposes of study, research, criticism or review, no part of this book may be reproduced, stored in a retrieval system, or transmitted in any form or by any means without prior written permission. All enquiries should be made to the publisher at the address above.

Any performance or public reading of *Running with Emus* is forbidden unless a licence has been received from the author or the author's agent. The purchase of this book in no way gives the purchaser the right to perform the play in public, whether by means of a staged production or a reading. All applications for public performance should be addressed to the author c/- Currency Press.

Typeset by Dean Nottle for Currency Press.
Cover image by Darren Gill.
Cover shows Julie Nihill and Sam Baxter.

Currency Press acknowledges the Traditional Owners of the Country on which we live and work. We pay our respects to all Aboriginal and Torres Strait Islander Elders, past and present.

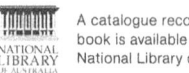

A catalogue record for this book is available from the National Library of Australia

Contents

RUNNING WITH EMUS   1

Theatre Program at the end of the playtext

'Hope is the thing with feathers'
Emily Dickinson

Running with Emus was launched on the verandah of the Tree Tops Scout Camp, Cohuna, Victoria, on 29 February 2020, followed by a season at La Mama Courthouse Theatre, Melbourne, from 11 March 2020, with the following cast:

PAT	Julie Nihill
KRYSTAL / RENEE	Elizabeth Sly
PIE	Gregory J Fryer
RAFFAELE / GOOSE	Sam Baxter
SPARRA / JIM	Kevin Dee

Director, Kim Durban
Designer, Adam (Gus) Powers

CHARACTERS

    PAT, Patricia Reilly, 76 years
    KRYSTAL, Pat's granddaughter, 38 years
    RAFFAELE, Italian prisoner of war (POW), 28 years
    JIM BOULDER, Mayor of Burridja, 58 years
    RENEE, local
    SPARRA, local, Anglo
    PIE, local, Indigenous
    GOOSE, local, farmer in a scooter/gopher with Australian flag

Ideally, the the play would be performed by six actors, but it could be performed by four. The actors who play Krystal, Raffaele and Jim could also play Sparra, Pie and Goose. The Chorus can be male or female.

SETTING

Burridja. A small town in the Malle, Victoria.

The action of the play takes place on a verandah on the edge of a red gum forest, in 2018.

This play went to press before the end of rehearsals and may differ from the play as performed.

SCENE 1

Dusk.

A verandah, crowded with things, including a table with an electric jug, mugs, binoculars, a small refrigerator. A single bed/couch in the middle of it all. A small barbecue off the verandah.

PAT *is taking photos with her phone. She zooms in on a floorboard, a window sill, birds (the audience).*

PAT: [*to the house*] Just you and me now, House. Stuffed to the rafters with mildew and memories. Wind whistles through the walls and rattles the window frames. Rain spills from the ceiling and pools on the beds.

When I was young, you were as tight as a drum, neat as a pin. Everything shipshape and proper. No breeze dared swell a curtain, no floorboard creak, no dust settle, no spill soaked to stain.

I've swept, vacuumed, polished, scrubbed, dusted, ironed, picked up, washed and tidied you my whole life. I know every curve, dimple, bruise and blemish—every patch of worn carpet, flake of peeling paint, every grain of red dust crammed into every crevice, every corner splay of spider's web, every chip on every cornice.

She settles into a chair.

Just us now. No-one bossing, nagging, wanting, needing, drinking, eating, dripping, groaning, pooing, weeing, sweating, vomiting, bleeding. No-one shouting, [*In her mother's voice*] Patricia, tidy your room. Patricia, the men are ready for their tea. Patricia, how many times do I have to tell you? Have you hung the washing, Patricia? [*A man's voice*] Pat, did you iron my blue shirt? Pat, what's for dinner? Pat, we're out of dunny paper! [*A child's voice*] Mum, I can't find my sport's uniform. But I've looked, Mum. I've looked everywhere. [*A child's voice*] But, Grummy, Granddad said I could have two pieces of chocolate cake. Why can't I? But why, Grummy? Why?

No more doors flinging open. Bags skidding across the floor, thudding into the wall.

She takes a few photos.

Time to document this delicious disorder. Wattle birds diving for bugs. Magpies hovering over squawking babies. Kookaburras chortling on the clothes line. Blue-eyed honeysuckers sharing figs with ants. Galahs waddling about in circles. Time to slap a few mosquitoes and doze off under the stars. Time to add my snore to the nocturnal concert of owl's toot and frog's burp.

We're closed to business, you and I. Your cupboards spilt their contents long ago. I still know which heap to excavate to unearth the 1954 *Women's Weekly*'s coverage of the Queen's visit to Australia. But why would I? Dust as thick as carpet. Peace and quiet. Time to mull over the past—to ruminate, revel and regret. No interruption. No argument. Time to lie back and sink slowly into the earth. What a rush it's all been.

> KRYSTAL *stomps onto the verandah. Her suitcase rolls against the wall.*

KRYSTAL: Grummy!

> PAT *sits up with a start.*

PAT: What the fuck?!

KRYSTAL: The bus took forever. I'm starving. Why don't they let you eat on the bus? I bet it's a racist thing—don't like the smell of garlic.

PAT: Krystal?

KRYSTAL: Sorry I'm so late. Anything to eat?

> *She tries to hug* PAT, *who stiffens.*

I told you I was coming.

PAT: Coming where?

KRYSTAL: I texted you from the bus.

PAT: You can't stay.

KRYSTAL: What?

PAT: There's no room.

KRYSTAL: There's a whole house.

PAT: It's full.

> KRYSTAL *tries to open the front door, but it bangs up against something.*

KRYSTAL: How do you open it?

PAT: You don't.

>KRYSTAL *notices the unmade bed on the verandah.*

KRYSTAL: Are you sleeping outside?
PAT: None of your business.
KRYSTAL: Jesus, Grummy. Don't you check your phone?

>KRYSTAL *tries to take* PAT*'s phone from her hand.* PAT *jerks her hand back.*

PAT: Don't touch my camera.
KRYSTAL: It's a phone.
PAT: I know that.
KRYSTAL: Are you okay, Grummy?
PAT: Why are you here?
KRYSTAL: I told you. In the email. I've been invited.
PAT: Not by me.
KRYSTAL: By the Refugee Support Group.
PAT: What's that when it's at home?
KRYSTAL: The Burridja Refugee Support—
PAT: Never heard of them.
KRYSTAL: They're writing a submission.
PAT: More fool them.
KRYSTAL: I'm the visiting expert.
PAT: On what? How to invade an old lady's home?
KRYSTAL: How to write a submission.
PAT: You think no-one in Burridja can do that?
KRYSTAL: It was all in the email. They want to make the Shire a Refugee Friendly Zone.
PAT: Why?
KRYSTAL: I volunteer at the Asylum Seeker Support Centre—in the city.
PAT: How long will it take?
KRYSTAL: What?
PAT: This submission thing.
KRYSTAL: There are lots of Friendly Zones in Victoria already.
PAT: You can stay at the motel.
KRYSTAL: Bendigo, Dandenong, Moreland, Bass Coast …
PAT: They have teddy bears.
KRYSTAL: Refugees can regenerate a small town's economy. It's a proven fact. The town of Nhill has the Karen people from Myanmar. They work at 'Luv-a-Duck'.

PAT: One on every bed.
KRYSTAL: Refugees?
PAT: Teddy bears.
KRYSTAL: Teddy bears?
PAT: At the motel.
KRYSTAL: I'm staying here. With you.
PAT: Air-conditioning in every room. We're having a heatwave.
KRYSTAL: [*looking around*] I can help you clear up.
PAT: Piss off.
KRYSTAL: What?
PAT: Don't touch my stuff.
KRYSTAL: Why are you being so nasty?
PAT: Why are you here?
KRYSTAL: Have you got a visitor?
PAT: Nope.
KRYSTAL: Who were you talking to?
PAT: No-one.
KRYSTAL: You know what they say about—
PAT: I was talking to my house. If you must know.
KRYSTAL: Your house?
PAT: Shirley Valentine talked to her wall.
KRYSTAL: Who's Shirley Valentine?
PAT: [*rolling her eyes*] Google it.
KRYSTAL: Does it answer?
PAT: It's a house.

SCENE 2

Chorus—SPARRA *and* PIE *sit on a bench,* GOOSE *in his scooter.*

GOOSE: Hot enough for you?
SPARRA: Gonna be forty-five on Sunday.
PIE: Not till after three.
GOOSE: Hot and windy.
PIE: Farmers won't be happy.
SPARRA: Are you happy, Goose?
GOOSE: What do you reckon?
SPARRA: Should be right in the morning.

PIE: Wait'll it hits forty.
SPARRA: Still cool in the house.
GOOSE: Not stuffy heat.
PIE: Like the city.
SPARRA: All that cement.
PIE: Shiny metal.
GOOSE: Suntraps.
SPARRA: Clogging up the roads.
PIE: Wouldn't live there for quids.
GOOSE: Could do with more rain.
SPARRA: Make the farmers happy.
GOOSE and PIE: [*together*] Never.

SCENE 3

Night.

PAT *is talking to the house, taking photos of door, window.*

RAFFAELE *observes from an obscure part of the stage.*

PAT: My mother was born here. My father drank and stormed here. I grew up here.

Father, uncles, husband, brothers, nephews and their friends, dumped hats, boots, bags, papers, cans, cups, plates, on your clean surfaces. Mother offered no instruction. She expected a girl to pop from the womb fully informed about domestic duties. In Eileen's house, you learned through trial and error, criticised at every turn. [*Eileen's voice*] 'What is the point of vacuuming if you don't clean the skirting boards?!'

My big sister wasn't having it. She put her foot down early. Lily wasn't going to live her life working her fingers to the bone trapped on a farm in the middle of nowhere. Not Lily. Lily's long gone. Lily spread her wings and left me grounded.

Beat.

My daughter played here. My husband died here. My granddaughter learned to walk here.

Beat.

Little Miss Upstart. Poking her nose in. Town doesn't need help. I don't need help. Bloody blow-in from down south. What would a newcomer know? Refugees in Burridja. What rubbish. Locals'll have a laugh. No use going to the Shire. Hitting your head against a brick wall.

 She stares at the house.

Where did she sleep? Back door's been stuck for months.
RAFFAELE: [*still unseen*] *Ha fatto la spesa.*
PAT: [*to the house*] What's that?
RAFFAELE: Girl is shopping.
PAT: [*to the house*] IGA closes at seven.
RAFFAELE: She goes this morning. *Stamattina.*
PAT: Did she touch anything? Those magazines are in chronological order.

  RAFFAELE *steps into view.*

RAFFAELE: Krystal not touch *giornali*.
PAT: Another one!
RAFFAELE: *Mi dispiace.* Sorry to frighten.
PAT: Who are you?
RAFFAELE: I am Raffaele. *Buonasera.*
PAT: She didn't say anything about a boyfriend.
RAFFAELE: Good evening, Patrizia.
PAT: [*taking his photo*] Mrs Reilly to you.
RAFFAELE: *Si, signora.*

  PAT *stares up at the sky.* RAFFAELE *follows her gaze.*

Grande nuvola di stelle.
PAT: Pardon?
RAFFAELE: Big cloud. Many star.
PAT: That's the Milky Way.
RAFFAELE: *Latte?*
PAT: Like spilled milk.
RAFFAELE: *Molto bello.*
PAT: Like a big snake.
RAFFAELE: I am frightened of *serpente*. *Ho paura.* Bluey say wear long socks and boots or snakes will bite.

PAT: Just stamp your feet. They like to feel you coming.
RAFFAELE: One day *mio amico* Gianni is screaming, pointing up, and we see *serpente* sliding in roof. We hate long-drop toilet. Smell so bad. Bluey say fill in hole. Dig new hole, move little house, fill in old hole. We hate. We kill snake with stick, but Bluey say, 'You should never kill snake, mate. Just make more snake.' Few days later and *presto!* more snake are coming. So we stop killing *serpenti*.
PAT: They say the Rainbow Serpent created the hills, the forest, the birds … Not that there's too many hills around here. Flat as a tack.
RAFFAELE: What is this story, Patrizia?
PAT: It's a Dreamtime story. The Serpent wriggled about all over the land and made the hills and mountains. And then …
RAFFAELE: *Sì?*
PAT: He ate a couple of boys.
RAFFAELE: *Mio dio!*
PAT: But when the Serpent was sleeping, the boys' family crept up and cut a hole in Serpent's stomach—and the boys turned into rosellas and flew away.
RAFFAELE: Rosella?
PAT: Rainbow birds.
RAFFAELE: *È buono.*
PAT: The Serpent was very angry.
RAFFAELE: *Naturalemente.*
PAT: He chased all the people. But they ran so fast they turned into kangaroos, wombats, lizards and magpies.
RAFFAELE: Why *serpente* is in sky now?
PAT: They say he's looking for a waterhole. [*She looks at* RAFFAELE.] What did you say your name was?
RAFFAELE: Raffaele.
PAT: I'll call you Raff.
RAFFAELE: *Va bene.*
PAT: Looks like it's clouding over. Might even get a bit of rain.

SCENE 4

Morning.
The sound of kookaburras.

PAT *is drinking coffee.* KRYSTAL *emerges, sleepy.*

KRYSTAL: Love the sound of rain on a tin roof.
PAT: That's just a sprinkle. Need a lot more. Coffee?

She pours KRYSTAL *a cup from the percolator.*

Hope you like it black.
KRYSTAL: I heard you talking in the night.
PAT: Little pigs have big ears.
KRYSTAL: I'm not a child.
PAT: You're my grandchild.
KRYSTAL: Talking to your house again?
PAT: To your boyfriend.
KRYSTAL: Don't have a boyfriend.
PAT: Your friend who is a boy.
KRYSTAL: I broke up with my girlfriend.
PAT: So that's why you're here.
KRYSTAL: I'm here to write a submission. I told you.
PAT: I believe you. Thousands wouldn't.
KRYSTAL: What do you and your house talk about?
PAT: I was talking to Raff.
KRYSTAL: The house has a name?
PAT: Don't be ridiculous.
KRYSTAL: I'm not the one talking to a house called Raff.
PAT: [*confused, irritated*] It's my house. I can talk to it. I can name it. I can burn it down if I want to.
KRYSTAL: Raff. Good name.

Beat. Kookaburras laugh.

PAT: Kookaburras are hysterical this morning, must be the rain.
KRYSTAL: They know I'm a square peg.
PAT: Whole town knows that by now.
KRYSTAL: I've got culture shock.
PAT: You know what to do.
KRYSTAL: Rents are sky-high in the city.
PAT: Compared to living here for free.
KRYSTAL: I can pay.
PAT: Show me the money.
KRYSTAL: I'm looking for work.

PAT: 'Visiting expert'? 'Girl with broken heart'? Or just 'Too broke to pay the rent'?
KRYSTAL: Maybe all three.
PAT: Don't settle in.
KRYSTAL: I can pay you.
PAT: When?
KRYSTAL: Tomorrow.
PAT: Know what they say about—?
KRYSTAL: I mean it.
PAT: Where did you sleep?
KRYSTAL: I can't sleep. I've got jet lag.
PAT: It's only a three-hour drive.
KRYSTAL: It's like another country. It's so hot. And dry. Huge dome of blue sky. Men in big hats and big dogs on the back of trucks. Everyone obsessed with sport. Yesterday, I walked past the bowling green, the tennis courts and the footy oval. Who needs all that space?
PAT: People who play with balls.
KRYSTAL: Then I get knocked over by this massive labrador.
PAT: That'd be Cow.
KRYSTAL: The dog is called 'Cow'?
PAT: Stupid mutt.
KRYSTAL: You have to smile at everyone. My face muscles are sore.
PAT: That's why I stay home.
KRYSTAL: When you cross the road—even if a car's a kilometre away and crawling—you wait. Today, an old guy saw me at the side of the road, waiting. What does he do?
PAT: He slows down.
KRYSTAL: Then he stops and waves me across. Then he watches me cross. Then he waves and smiles. Then I wave and smile back. Then he drives off.
PAT: Life in the fast lane.
KRYSTAL: In the car, you raise one finger off the steering wheel.
PAT: [*lifting her index finger*] Nonchalantly.
KRYSTAL: The town's about the size of a shopping mall, but everyone drives.
PAT: Including you. In *my* car.
KRYSTAL: I saw a woman pull out from the IGA, drive less than fifty metres and stop at the bank.

PAT: You can always get a park.
KRYSTAL: So this woman, Renee—
PAT: Mother of Cow.
KRYSTAL: —asks me if I'm staying out by Reilly's Bridge. I tell her I am and she says, 'You must be Krystal'.
PAT: They know everything.
KRYSTAL: I asked if she was a local. She said, / 'Born and bred'.
PAT: / Born and bred.
KRYSTAL: Then she asked if I played golf. 'I'm not really a sporty person,' I said.
PAT: Blasphemy.
KRYSTAL: What's going to happen when I say I'm vegetarian?
PAT: Better keep quiet about that one.
KRYSTAL: 'What about tennis?' she says, quick as a flash. 'You haven't lived until you've played on grass.' I shake my head, so she digs around in her pocket and pulls out this pamphlet.

> KRYSTAL *hands the pamphlet to* PAT.

PAT: [*reading*] 'Breakfast with the Birds'.
KRYSTAL: I'm thinking, bor-ring.
PAT: You can have breakfast with the birds right here—on this verandah.

> *She offers* KRYSTAL *binoculars.*

We've got galahs, rosellas, magpies, honeysuckers, choughs, kites, blackbirds, wattle birds, little fairy-wrens … all here—in my backyard. Want more, just take a few steps into the forest.
KRYSTAL: Renee's picking me up five-thirty Sunday morning.

SCENE 5

Day.

PAT *is curled on the bed, dozing.*

The sound of a gate opening. She sits up, straightens her clothes. JIM *enters, carrying a box of groceries.*

JIM: How you going?
PAT: You the delivery boy now?
JIM: I was at the supermarket—saw a box with your name on it.

PAT: Not exactly 'on your way'.

    JIM *puts the box down.*

JIM: How you doing?
PAT: I'm good.
JIM: Sleeping outside?
PAT: Bit of fresh air.
JIM: Never did anyone any harm.

    JIM *looks around.*

    PAT *puts a few things in the fridge.*

PAT: Glass of water?
JIM: I'm right.
PAT: You want something else?
JIM: People are asking about you.
PAT: People?
JIM: You just disappear.
PAT: I'm retired.
JIM: Are you okay?
PAT: Jesus.
JIM: People are worried.
PAT: What people?
JIM: I'm worried, Pat.
PAT: You?
JIM: Yeah.
PAT: How are you coping, Jim?
JIM: Me?
PAT: Without Sooz.
JIM: I'm good.
PAT: Well, that's settled. We're both good.
JIM: You coming to the Reconciliation March? I can pick you up.
PAT: I can drive myself.
JIM: School kids are gonna do a dance. Auntie Dawn's doing the smoking ceremony. Sure you don't want a lift? [*He looks at the house.*] Want me to fix that door?
PAT: No, thanks.

    Beat.

JIM: See you at the march then?
PAT: Have to think about it.
JIM: You could say a few words.
PAT: You're the mayor, Jim. [*Looking at an imaginary watch*] Don't you have cows to milk?
JIM: Righto, Pat. See you next week.

> JIM *leaves.*

> PAT *lies down again.*

SCENE 6

Night.

PAT *is sleeping.*

KRYSTAL *staggers in, her head bleeding. She's a little drunk.*

PAT *stands and guides* KRYSTAL *to a chair, inspects her forehead. Takes a photo of it.*

PAT: How did you get home?
KRYSTAL: Got a lift.
PAT: Who from?
KRYSTAL: Some bloke from the pub.
PAT: Some bloke.

> PAT *takes a few more photos.*

KRYSTAL: Stop that.
PAT: Forensic evidence.

> *She boils the kettle, fills a bowl, bathes the wound.*

Bit of hot salty water, fix anything. Hold still.
KRYSTAL: [*flinching*] I'm fragile.
PAT: Like a Mallee bull.
KRYSTAL: Think I'm going to be sick.
PAT: Not on me, you won't.
KRYSTAL: Might have overdone it.
PAT: You think?

> *She takes another photo of the wound.*

How did you go?

KRYSTAL: They didn't listen.
PAT: You should listen to your grandmother. [*Patting her forehead*] There. That should do it.
KRYSTAL: It was worth a shot.
PAT: Waste of time. And energy. What happened?
KRYSTAL: We had a meeting. It was stacked with rednecks.
PAT: What happened to your head?
KRYSTAL: That was at the hotel after. Things got nasty. A bloke hit me.
PAT: Hit you?
KRYSTAL: He shoved me and I fell, cracked my head on the piano.
PAT: Did you call the police?
KRYSTAL: I'll be okay.

SCENE 7

Dusk.

PAT *is having a glass of red wine.*

A flock of corellas scream overhead.

RAFFAELE *appears.*

RAFFAELE: What is screaming?
PAT: You again.
RAFFAELE: [*blocking his ears*] *Troppo rumoroso.*
PAT: Just corellas. Little cockatoos.
RAFFAELE: Like naughty schoolboys. Screaming for screaming. *Guardami!* Look at me!
PAT: No point whispering. It's a big country.
RAFFAELE: [*pointing*] What is bird with hook for mouth?
PAT: Ibis.
RAFFAELE: [*pointing*] *Quello?*
PAT: That one? That's a kite. A type of hawk.
RAFFAELE: Like kite make with paper. Fly in circle.
PAT: It's looking for mice. One took Mrs Scott's chihuahua a few years back.

    RAFFAELE *is puzzled.*

Her little dog.
RAFFAELE: *Vero?*

PAT: She ran after it, waving a broom. It dropped the dog in the dam.
RAFFAELE: Chihuahua live?
PAT: A few stitches.
RAFFAELE: I like *il canguro*. Face like friendly mouse.
PAT: They have a nasty kick.
RAFFAELE: *Vero?*
PAT: We have drop bears too. *Thylarctos Plummetus.*
RAFFAELE: Bluey tell me this joke. I know no drop bear, Patrizia.
PAT: Mrs Reilly to you.
RAFFAELE: *Sì, signora.*

   They stare out at the sky.

   I look for North Star. *Ma non c'è.*
PAT: Wrong side of the world. [*Pointing*] There's the Southern Cross. The Saucepan. [*Explaining*] That's Orion up north, but upside down.

   They hear the booming of an emu.

RAFFAELE: [*nervous*] What is big drum?
PAT: [*listening*] That?
RAFFAELE: Like ghost lost in forest.
PAT: Just an emu.
RAFFAELE: [*excited*] Big bird with blue neck?
PAT: Must be breeding season.
RAFFAELE: I love this bird. *L'adoro.*
PAT: The female only has to drop the egg. Then she's off. Dad sticks around to look after his baby.
RAFFAELE: Em-you.
PAT: I've tried to take a photo, but she's too fast.
RAFFAELE: [*scratching*] *Ho caldo, Signora Patrizia.*
PAT: Another hot one tomorrow.
RAFFAELE: At home, when we have hot, we eat *gelati*. We make *la passegiata*. Women put lipstick, scarf. I have good shirt. We walk. We eat ice-cream. *Cioccolato, limone, pistaccio, fragola* ... [*Licking his lips, a sob escapes.*] I cannot taste. I cannot forget and I cannot remember.
PAT: Why don't you go home, eat ice-cream, look at the North Star?
RAFFAELE: *Impossibile.*
PAT: Why hang round an old lady?

SCENE 8

Chorus—PIE, SPARRA, GOOSE.

They are queuing—jostling one another. GOOSE *still in his scooter.*

PIE: Outta me way, Sparra.
SPARRA: Queue up. Wait your turn.
GOOSE: I got here first.
SPARRA: Form a crocodile.
PIE: Crocs don't queue. Straight up the bank, grab your ankle.
GOOSE: First in, first served.
SPARRA: Wait in line.
PIE: Yous never stood in no queue.
SPARRA: It's the civilised way.
GOOSE: At the footie.
SPARRA: At the butchers.
GOOSE: At the bus stop.
PIE: Supermarket check-out.
SPARRA: There was a queue at the Tattslotto this morning.
GOOSE: Tell me about it.

SCENE 9

Morning.

PAT *is drinking coffee. There's an aluminium percolator on the small BBQ.*

KRYSTAL *enters with a carton of milk.*

PAT: How's the head?
KRYSTAL: Think I've got concussion.
PAT: There's coffee.
KRYSTAL: [*holding her head*] I could sue.
PAT: Go to the clinic first. It's just up the road.
KRYSTAL: Everything's just up the road.

> PAT *pushes* KRYSTAL*'s hair off the wound. She takes another photo.*

PAT: Ask for Dr Ramess.

KRYSTAL: Ramess? Is he Indian?
PAT: I think she's Egyptian.
KRYSTAL: An Egyptian doctor—in Burridja.
PAT: You'll love the clinic. It's our multicultural centre.

KRYSTAL pours coffee.

How long you staying?
KRYSTAL: I just got here.
PAT: Does Alison know you're here?
KRYSTAL: Mum's got her own life. She's *Elena* now.

She drinks.

Best coffee in town.
PAT: Sit back and smell the Acacia montana.
KRYSTAL: Smell what?
PAT: The wattle.
KRYSTAL: Mum always said that. 'Smell the wattle.' We never had any wattle.

KRYSTAL sneezes.

PAT: Wattle made Alison sneeze.
KRYSTAL: Elena.

Beat.

Guess who's in the Refugee Support Group? Renee.
PAT: Renee Watts. School principal. Of course she is.
KRYSTAL: She was brilliant at the shire meeting. Should be in parliament.

Re-enactment:

RENEE: *Our kids think it's okay to walk out of a class because the teacher has an accent. They can't handle a different way of speaking. It has to be coming from their parents. It's rude—and it's lazy. Our teachers leave. We need doctors, desperately, but the doctors don't stay. Locals won't even try to pronounce their names. If the shire votes today to become a Refugee Friendly Zone, it will lead the way to a more open-minded community.*

PAT: Bet they loved that.
KRYSTAL: Then the bloody mayor pipes up—
PAT: Jim.

KRYSTAL: Racist, bigoted, xenophobic Jim Boulder.
JIM: *I've got nothing against refugees, but who's going to pay for all this? Where are they all from? Are they screened? Are they on the waiting list? Have they jumped the queue? Are they illegal immigrants? How do we know what we're getting?*

    KRYSTAL *lifts her hand to speak—as if she's in school.*

[Nodding at KRYSTAL*] We have some people here to support the motion. Go ahead. From the gallery.*
KRYSTAL: *Krystal Donahue, Refugee Support Group.*
JIM: *Thanks for coming.*
KRYSTAL: *We can help with the transition.*
JIM: *We?*
KRYSTAL: *There's an infrastructure already in place. The Neighbourhood House has a bank of computers and training courses. The Burridja Health Centre offers counselling. You have a medical clinic, schools, churches ... a hospital.*
JIM: *It didn't work in Colac.*
KRYSTAL: *They didn't have the jobs.*
PAT: We don't have the jobs.
KRYSTAL: *It's only an 'in spirit' agreement at this stage.*
JIM: *You have to provide support—counselling, English lessons. Someone has to take them down to the shops, make sure they know how to buy food. We don't want a doctor sitting home watching a tele he doesn't understand. Wasting his time looking for non-existent work.*
KRYSTAL: *We don't have to do it all at once.*
JIM: *Problems with their mental health.*
KRYSTAL: Then Renee jumped in again.
RENEE: *A couple from Brazil are working at the supermarket in Yiari. The community mentored them. The men came first—then they brought their families. Some farmers sponsored them. They needed the labour. Filipinos work at the piggery. Their kids go to the Catholic school. The school stays open. Everybody benefits.*
JIM: *What about our own youth? The homeless. If we focus on refugees, what have we got left for the locals? What does 'becoming a Refugee Friendly Zone' really mean anyway?*
RENEE: *It means having a commitment in spirit to embracing difference and understanding other cultures.*

JIM: *[laughing] And we won't have to do anything? Nothing at all? Pull the other one.*
RENEE: *It would connect us to the rest of the world. Improve the existing infrastructure.*
JIM: *So it's not just signing a piece of paper. It'll come out of our pockets. The pockets of local government. We're losing our locals as it is. Kids all moving to the big towns and the city. How are we going to integrate these people into the community?*
RENEE: *It's just a gesture at this stage.*
JIM: *Look at the problems in Melbourne. Hordes of young African men carjacking, breaking into houses, bashing defenceless old women. Do you want that here?*
KRYSTAL: That's when I had to pipe up again. He made me so mad. *[Losing her cool] That's a media blow-up. Statistics show white men on ice commit more crime.*
PAT: Should leave it to Renee. I reckon.
KRYSTAL: *[agreeing]* She's so calm—and articulate.
PAT: You'll never die wondering what's on her mind.
JIM: *They come here, take all the resources, go on the dole ...*
RENEE: *I think you'll find it's in line with your Council Plan.*
JIM: *We need to look at the whole picture.*
RENEE: *In Yiari a local woman has set up a food outlet—selling Filipino food. She shops down in Melbourne. Swan Hill has Afghans and Harmony Day.*
JIM: *We've got Harmony Day here too. Had it at the Infant Welfare Centre. There were about eight Indians.*
KRYSTAL: *[to* PAT*]* A couple of thousand Anglos in town. They rake up eight Indians and call it Harmony Day.
JIM: *They wore their saris.*
KRYSTAL: People won't buy petrol at the top garage. They think they're being overrun—by eight Indians.
JIM: *Indian women are so graceful.*
KRYSTAL: Not every Indian woman is graceful. Not every Australian has a kangaroo in their backyard. And, much as I hate to admit it, not all men are bastards.
PAT: But all magpies are black and white. Some generalisations are true.
JIM: *[overlapping from the re-enactment] We should be helping white South African farmers. They're under attack. They share our culture.*

They can assimilate. People around here aren't racist. They're just not used to them.

PAT: All ballerinas stand on their toes.
KRYSTAL: Not fat little girls who never wanted to go in the first place.
PAT: Did Alison tell you about that?
KRYSTAL: She tells everyone.

SCENE 10

Chorus—PIE, SPARRA, GOOSE.

GOOSE: People you see when you haven't got a gun.
PIE: Missed me, mate?
SPARRA: What do you know?
PIE: Not much. Wouldn't tell you if I did.
GOOSE: Bumped into B.J. out the back.
PIE: The people smuggler.
SPARRA: B.J.?
GOOSE: Got that Japanese wife.
SPARRA: Filipino.
GOOSE: Near enough.
PIE: Got himself a missus from Bali.
SPARRA: I think she's Filipino.
PIE: Near enough.
GOOSE: A lot them Filipinos women, skipping the queue—finding husbands.
SPARRA: Aussie men finding wives.
GOOSE: People smugglers. Either way.
PIE: Too lazy to learn how to cook after his missus died.
SPARRA: Hard to know who's exploiting who.
PIE: *Whom*.
GOOSE: Hoity-toity.
PIE: Taking our jobs.
SPARRA: Filipinos are migrants too.
GOOSE: Queue jumping.
SPARRA: Want to help out their families back home.
GOOSE: With our money.
PIE: You're a boat people. You're both boat people.

GOOSE: Don't start.
SPARRA: Pie has a point.
GOOSE: This'll be good.
SPARRA: We came on a boat. We sought refuge. England was too wet, too cold. We wanted sun and surf and a big blue sky.
PIE: Not much surf in the creek, mate.
SPARRA: But look at the sky.

SCENE 11

Day.

The verandah. KRYSTAL *is eating pasta.*

PAT: How was your breakfast—with the birds?
KRYSTAL: Brilliant.
PAT: Don't know why you have to go all the way to Henty Swamp. Got the forest right here. Bush chorus twice a day.
KRYSTAL: There were busloads—at six in the morning.
PAT: People like birds.
KRYSTAL: Who knew?
PAT: Your grandmother.
KRYSTAL: One lot were from Game Victoria.
PAT: Murderers.
KRYSTAL: The other from the Coalition Against Duck Hunting. But after a bit of an argument and a cup of tea everyone picked up their binoculars.
PAT: Well?
KRYSTAL: Well what?
PAT: What did you see?
KRYSTAL: [*consulting her pamphlet*] I saw a freckled duck, two types of cormorant, lots of different ibis, a royal spoonbill, a Eurasian coot and heaps of black-winged stilts.
PAT: Any pelicans?
KRYSTAL: I also saw a bunch of pelicans drift by. They were clacking their beaks. Renee told me they do that to herd the fish.
PAT: She an expert on birds too? How many pelicans?
KRYSTAL: Maybe twenty. They were amazing, Grummy. What's the collective noun for pelicans?

PAT: Might have to visit this swamp.

    PAT *peers over* KRYSTAL*'s shoulder at her plate.*

KRYSTAL: Want some?

PAT: What is it?

KRYSTAL: It's out of a packet.

PAT: What is?

KRYSTAL: Potato gnocchi. They sell it in the supermarket.

PAT: Here in Burridja?

KRYSTAL: [*nodding*] At the IGA.

PAT: Wonders will never cease.

KRYSTAL: You taught me to make pasta when I was little. Real pasta, with flour and everything. Rolling the dough into little balls. Who taught you?

PAT: Not rocket science.

KRYSTAL: You said, 'Time to get our hands dirty'.

PAT: After Mum's funeral.

KRYSTAL: I stood on a chair.

PAT: Flour all over the kitchen.

KRYSTAL: Grandma didn't like mess.

PAT: Tell me about it.

KRYSTAL: She'd be bonkers now. Look at the place.

PAT: Took me a while.

KRYSTAL: You've got so much stuff.

    Beat.

Do you mind if I clear out the back room?

PAT: Yes.

KRYSTAL: Yes, I can?

PAT: Yes, I mind.

KRYSTAL: Just the sleep-out.

PAT: Go home. Live with Alison.

KRYSTAL: I'm a grown-up.

PAT: So you say.

KRYSTAL: Just for a couple of months. I'll pay rent.

PAT: With what?

KRYSTAL: I'm going for a job.

PAT: Doing what?

KRYSTAL: Milking.
PAT: What do you know about milking?
KRYSTAL: Can't I learn?
PAT: You'll have get up in the dark.
KRYSTAL: I'll set my alarm.
PAT: Where are you sleeping?
KRYSTAL: Round the back.
PAT: Inside?
KRYSTAL: Grandma Eileen gave me spaghetti on toast. From a tin.
PAT: Grandma Eileen thought instant coffee was exotic.
KRYSTAL: She liked her tea.
PAT: [*holding up an imaginary cup, pinkie raised*] In a china cup.
KRYSTAL: [*holding up an imaginary cup, pinkie raised*] With a matching saucer and plate.
PAT: Mum was more English than the English. Poor thing.
KRYSTAL: Why 'poor thing'?
PAT: She had a nervous breakdown.
KRYSTAL: Grandma Eileen?
PAT: That's what they called it. Said she couldn't cope with the heat.
KRYSTAL: I've seen the photos—with that frilly umbrella.
PAT: Always had that parasol. They locked her up.
KRYSTAL: Grandma?
PAT: Must have been the shock—all the way from Manchester to the Mallee.
KRYSTAL: Locked up?
PAT: Somewhere in the city—Kew?
KRYSTAL: Kew Asylum. The loony bin.
PAT: Before I was born.
KRYSTAL: Explains a lot.
PAT: Does it?
KRYSTAL: She was so rigid. Like her life depended on hanging the washing right.
PAT: Socks in pairs, pegged by the toes. Colour co-ordinated.
KRYSTAL: She ironed the sheets.

Beat.

PAT: Might have been Lily.

KRYSTAL: Lily?
PAT: Taught me to make gnocchi.
KRYSTAL: Great Auntie Lily?
PAT: My big sister. She ran off.
KRYSTAL: Mum told me. Where did she run to?
PAT: Dunno. It was easy to disappear back then.

SCENE 12

Chorus—PIE, SPARRA, GOOSE.

PIE: You one of those intellectual types, Sparra?
GOOSE: A smart fart.
PIE: La-dee-dah.
SPARRA: Ah, the arrogance of the ignorant.
GOOSE: Who you calling dumb?
SPARRA: You've got a bit of a chip.
GOOSE: What's that, Sparra?
SPARRA: [*tapping his shoulder*] Chip.
PIE: Only good chip is a hot chip.
GOOSE: Got no bloomin' chip. Shut up about the chip.
PIE: Keep it down, Goose.
SPARRA: You don't know how much you don't know until you know.
GOOSE: That how they talk at you-knee?
SPARRA: Your chip is showing.
PIE: Watch out for seagulls, Goose. They love a good chip.
SPARRA: Just because I've got a decent vocabulary.
GOOSE: La-dee-dah.
SPARRA: I might have a few more words to play with.
PIE: Might.
SPARRA: But I've never ridden a motorbike.

    PIE *and* GOOSE *pause to consider this turn in the conversation.*

Why haven't I ridden a motorbike, Pie?
PIE: Dunno.
SPARRA: Maybe because I feel intimidated. Maybe I feel intimidated because you're such a very good motorbike rider.
PIE: I am pretty good.

SPARRA: But I don't tell you to stop riding.
PIE: Like to see you try.
SPARRA: Know why I don't I tell you to stop?
PIE: Spit it out.
SPARRA: I choose to be impressed rather than envious.
GOOSE: Can't help yourself, can you, Sparra?
PIE: La-dee-dah.

SCENE 13

Day.

KRYSTAL: We're writing another submission. There's an election coming up—hopefully there'll be a turnover in council. Get rid of bloody Jim.
PAT: I wouldn't count on it.
KRYSTAL: How's this?

> *She refers to her notes.*

'It's timely that we demonstrate a commitment to create an inclusive, cultural and religiously diverse community by signing a public declaration to acknowledge and welcome refugees.'
PAT: You swallow a dictionary?
KRYSTAL: Don't play dumb.
PAT: Muslims are anti-woman, you know.
KRYSTAL: Where did that come from?
PAT: Don't you support women's rights?
KRYSTAL: That's rubbish.
PAT: Women covered in black, walking behind their man.
KRYSTAL: Catholics keep their women barefoot and pregnant.
PAT: Can't see their faces.
KRYSTAL: Catholic nuns have to marry God, an imaginary man.
PAT: Locked in the house, not allowed to work or go to school. Can't even drive.
KRYSTAL: It's not so different here in Burridja.
PAT: We can drive.
KRYSTAL: 'Ladies bring a plate' is hardly liberated. Can't see Jim stepping up with his plate of fudge.
PAT: I never take a plate.

KRYSTAL: You never go out.
PAT: Where are you going to put them?
KRYSTAL: Who?
PAT: These refugees.
KRYSTAL: It's just an agreement in spirit at this stage.
PAT: Know why it's so peaceful around here? Because we've got none of that 'cultural and religious diversity'.
KRYSTAL: Burridja is in the middle of an ice epidemic. The service station was robbed last week.
PAT: Which one?
KRYSTAL: Does it matter?
PAT: I just wondered.
KRYSTAL: You want to know if it's the one run by Indians.
PAT: I do not.
KRYSTAL: Yes, you do.
PAT: Was anyone hurt?
KRYSTAL: I don't think so.
PAT: Why do you want to believe I'm a racist?
KRYSTAL: I don't.
PAT: You think because a few people in town are frightened of change, everyone's a racist.
KRYSTAL: I do not.
PAT: You like feeling superior.
KRYSTAL: I do not.
PAT: Put you in the forest—you'll soon run out of words.

SCENE 14

Night.

PAT *and* RAFFAELE *sit companionably on the verandah,* PAT *sips wine.*

RAFFAELE: One day I am late for school. I run fast through *piazza*. All around me is market, *bancarelli*—tables with vegetables, fish, meat. This day I run too fast. I knock into *la pasticceria*. All the pastry is running to the *pavimento*. Everyone screaming. *Che disastro!* Bread is *sporco*, dirty. The man who make bread, Signor Giordano, *il panettiere*, he run after me. He catch my arm. I tell him I late for school. I tell him sorry. *Mi dispiace, signor.* He slap my face. *Così!*

He slaps himself.

Aiuto! I scream. Help! *Aiuto!* Signor Giordano's *moglie*, his wife, she screaming, '*Smettila!* Stop! Look what you do this poor boy.' Suddenly the signor, he drop me. *La donna* screaming. 'You break his arm in two pieces.' He say, *'Non è culpa mio'*. She slap him. *Così!*

He slaps himself.

My arm, she is on fire. But I am hero. At school everyone love me. Everyone in my village know this story. Everyone.

Beat.

No-one know nothing here. No-one know Signor Giordano break my arm. No-one know *mio fratello, mie sorelle, mia mamma* … Know only Italian chicken, wog man in red *pantaloni*.

PAT: I know something. The baker broke your arm when you were a boy. You miss your home town.
RAFFAELE: [*wiping his eyes*] *Grazie, Patrizia.*
PAT: [*raising her glass*] To the wog man in the red pants.

SCENE 15

Day.

PAT *and* KRYSTAL *sit on the verandah.*

PAT: We're not racist. We're just not used to them.
KRYSTAL: That's what Jim says.
PAT: We haven't had many foreigners in Burridja.
KRYSTAL: Bullshit.
PAT: Language.
KRYSTAL: You can talk.
PAT: It's my verandah.
KRYSTAL: What about the 'Balts'?
PAT: During the war?
KRYSTAL: Didn't some of them stick around?
PAT: 'Johnny-me-fix' bought the garage. His son fixes my car.
KRYSTAL: They weren't all from Baltic countries.
PAT: They were *all* our enemies. Internees.

KRYSTAL: Locked up at the old scout camp in the forest: Hungarians, Germans, Japanese …
PAT: Someone's done her homework.
KRYSTAL: I've been to the Historic Society.
PAT: Then you'll know there were P.O.W.s. Prisoners of—
KRYSTAL: Thousands of Italians captured in North Africa. The British didn't know where to put them.
PAT: They worked on farms around here.
KRYSTAL: There's a file called 'Enemy Aliens'.
PAT: We've got Chinese.
KRYSTAL: [*agreeing*] They run the takeaway.
PAT: 'Chinese Trev's'.
KRYSTAL: Why do you call it that?
PAT: Trev sold it to a Chinese family.
KRYSTAL: What's their name? The Chinese family.
PAT: Where's your sense of humour?
KRYSTAL: The Chinese have been here since the gold rush.
PAT: Not this lot.
KRYSTAL: Since then we've had Italians, Greeks, Lebanese, Vietnamese, Sri Lankan, Iraqis, Sudanese …
PAT: Not many of them came to Burridja.
KRYSTAL: Who ran the market gardens?
PAT: Wogs.
KRYSTAL: Stop saying that.
PAT: It's just a bit of fun. They don't mind.
KRYSTAL: Any Muslims?
PAT: They're building a mosque in Bendigo.
KRYSTAL: I know.
PAT: They say they breed like rabbits.
KRYSTAL: [*appalled*] What?
PAT: It was on the radio. Someone on the radio said it. Not me.
KRYSTAL: They used to say that about the Catholics.
PAT: What?
KRYSTAL: They breed like rabbits.
PAT: I didn't breed like any rabbit.
KRYSTAL: The pope wanted you to have ten children.
PAT: I only had Alison.

KRYSTAL: Elena.
PAT: Why do you keep saying that?
KRYSTAL: Because Mum's changed her name.
PAT: Big kids at the bus stop chanting, 'Catholic dog, sitting on a log, eating maggots out of a frog'. I was scared to walk home.
KRYSTAL: But you didn't mind. It was all in fun.
PAT: [*annoyed*] At least the Christians don't go round killing people for Jesus.
KRYSTAL: The Nazis were Christians, Grummy. Religion is the problem—not refugees. And rampant capitalism. If the rich paid a bit of tax, shared their trillions, we could support all the refugees and have plenty left. We spend it all on keeping them locked up on Manus Island. I'm ashamed to be Australian. We have to stop thinking about borders.
PAT: No wonder someone hit you. I want to hit you.
KRYSTAL: Aung San Suu Kyi ignores the burning of Rohingya villages in Myanmar. Turkey denies the genocide of the Armenians. We deny the massacre of the Aborigines. How come people can see other countries' atrocities, but they're so blind to their own?
PAT: Same reason I can see all your faults, but you think you're perfect.
KRYSTAL: Even the UN is talking about us. We're a disgrace.
PAT: Why do you care?
KRYSTAL: What happened to kindness? Sharing? Making a casserole for the new neighbours?
PAT: They might be vegetarians.
KRYSTAL: Some people seem to have no right to be on this planet. They've escaped for their lives, but all doors are shut. A country can go downhill so fast. It could happen here. Who would we turn to? Indonesia? New Zealand?

> *Beat.*

Sometimes I feel like a refugee.
PAT: Don't be ridiculous.
KRYSTAL: I know I'm lucky. I'm a citizen in a peaceful, democratic country. I'm not trudging through mud, carrying my life on my back. Or cooped up in a detention centre. But I'm struggling. I always seem to be outside, looking in.
PAT: You've got a broken heart. That's all.

KRYSTAL: I'm thirty-eight and I can't—
PAT: You've got me.
KRYSTAL: You don't seem very pleased to see me.
PAT: [*pulling her in and kissing her forehead*] I'm just a grumpy old Grummy. Got a lot on my mind.
KRYSTAL: Like what?
PAT: [*pushing her away*] Like how I can photograph that superb fairy-wren when it keeps jumping all over the place.
KRYSTAL: Are you storing your photos somewhere?
PAT: Why?
KRYSTAL: Would you like me to file them for you? Make a few videos?
PAT: I'm tired of storing things for later.
KRYSTAL: Why take photos?
PAT: It helps me concentrate.

  Beat.

KRYSTAL: You should come to the movie. There'll be amazing food.
PAT: I'm not hungry.
KRYSTAL: From all over the world: baklava, sushi, Afghan dips, nasi goreng …
PAT: I've had it with people. I'm with the birds now.
KRYSTAL: … spanakopita, pizza … you like pizza.
PAT: When will they make their decision? The shire.
KRYSTAL: The decision's made.
PAT: You might be wrong.
KRYSTAL: The mayor was at the pub. Spouting off. He'd had a few. 'No way that's going through,' he said, 'No fucking way.' Bloody Jim Boulder. I call him Mr Pebble.
PAT: Mr Pebble the one who punched you?

  KRYSTAL *shrugs.*

I'll have a word.
KRYSTAL: I can fight my own battles.
PAT: Looks like it.

SCENE 16

Chorus—PIE, SPARRA, GOOSE.

GOOSE: Where you off to, Pie?
PIE: Gotta get home to watch 'Border Security'.
SPARRA: What do you watch that crap for?
PIE: Dunno.
SPARRA: Make you feel safe?
PIE: Dunno.
SPARRA: Seeing foreigners getting caught with chicken feet in their suitcase?
GOOSE: Chicken feet's okay—it's just a fine for chicken feet.
SPARRA: You watch it too, Goose?
PIE: [*to* SPARRA] You must've seen it, Sparra, or you wouldn't know about the chicken feet.
GOOSE: Reckon they'll send her back?
PIE: Who?
GOOSE: One with the purple hair. She's got no money. How can she be a tourist? Never even heard of the Harbour Bridge.
PIE: Dunno.
GOOSE: Says she's visiting friends.
PIE: Doesn't even know where they live.

SCENE 17

Dusk.

PAT *is sitting.* KRYSTAL *appears.*

KRYSTAL: I got the job.
PAT: Doing what?
KRYSTAL: I'm a Relief Milker. Actually, I'm a Trainee Milker planning on becoming a Relief Milker, then maybe a Contract Milker.
PAT: A career pathway.
KRYSTAL: It's so noisy. And smelly. Poo everywhere.
PAT: City girl lands on earth.
KRYSTAL: The cows move round this 'U' shape and we stand in the middle, low down, looking right at their swollen udders.
PAT: A herringbone dairy.
KRYSTAL: Some of the bigger dairies are like a merry-go-round. The cows hop on and go for a ride.
PAT: A rotary.

KRYSTAL: I was just getting the hang of it today when a heifer jumped right up into the bale where they're eating. I screamed.
PAT: Helpful.
KRYSTAL: She sort of scurried along the side—got herself down.
PAT: The luck of the Irish.
KRYSTAL: A heifer is a young girl cow.
PAT: [*rolling her eyes*] Whose dairy?
KRYSTAL: I love cows. They're so placid.
PAT: One day milking. Give it time.
KRYSTAL: Have you seen their eyelashes, Grummy? You just have to send out your love and they come to you.
PAT: Where's this dairy?
KRYSTAL: You can scratch behind their ears. Some of them are stubborn. Jim calls the stubborn ones 'yabbies'.
PAT: Jim.
KRYSTAL: 'Cause they won't go in—they scuttle backwards like a yabbie.
PAT: Thought you hated Jim.
KRYSTAL: Don't have to agree on politics to work in the pit.
PAT: Wait till the cows start shitting on your head.
KRYSTAL: They don't poo while they're letting go milk.
PAT: That what he told you?
KRYSTAL: Do they?

> PAT *shrugs*.

I have to get up early tomorrow.
PAT: Don't wake me.
KRYSTAL: I'll set my alarm.
PAT: Not that stupid tooting train. Thought it was coming through the house.
KRYSTAL: Okay.
PAT: Or the barking dog.
KRYSTAL: How about crickets?

> *She plays crickets as she heads off to bed.*

SCENE 18

Night.

PAT *is preparing for bed.* RAFFAELE *is sitting on the steps of the verandah.*

PAT: Sometimes I think she's going to talk to me for the rest of my life.
RAFFAELE: She is full of passion and fury. I like this girl.
PAT: I'm busy.
RAFFAELE: She is like you. *Vuole cambiare il mondo.* She want to change the world.
PAT: I'm tired of playing ladies, looking after everyone else. It's my time—my turn. [*A sudden rush of Italian*] È il mio momento, il mio turno.

    KRYSTAL *enters.* RAFFAELE *exits.*

KRYSTAL: I didn't know you spoke Italian.
PAT: I don't.
KRYSTAL: What was that then?
PAT: Mind your beeswax.

    Beat.

Have you been drinking?
KRYSTAL: Yes.
PAT: Cows don't stop for hangovers.
KRYSTAL: [*noticing the glass of red wine*] I'm not the only one.
PAT: I don't have to get up in the dark.
KRYSTAL: That recycle bin is full of bottles.
PAT: I forgot to put the bin out.
KRYSTAL: For six months?
PAT: Why am I defending myself?
KRYSTAL: You feel guilty.
PAT: You're out there knocking it back. Staggering back at all hours in the dark. Who are you drinking with anyway? I thought the whole town hated you.
KRYSTAL: Not everyone.
PAT: [*lying down*] I'm sleeping now.
KRYSTAL: Your bed is in the communal area. People are going to talk to you.
PAT: My verandah.
KRYSTAL: [*sitting down on the bed*] Do you remember the White Australia Policy?
PAT: She's off again.
KRYSTAL: I'd never get in.

PAT: You're already here.
KRYSTAL: I've got olive skin.
PAT: Bit of Irish gypsy.
KRYSTAL: I'm much darker than Akari. She's Japanese.
PAT: Asians are yellow.
KRYSTAL: O. M. G!
PAT: What?
KRYSTAL: You didn't just say that.
PAT: What about the Yellow Peril?
KRYSTAL: What's that?
PAT: There was a red under every bed.
KRYSTAL: Red, yellow, white ... your generation is obsessed with colours. Azra has whiter skin than me and she's Turkish.
PAT: Azra?
KRYSTAL: She worked at the café with me. My girlfriend.
PAT: The one who left you?
KRYSTAL: Not exactly.
PAT: You left her?
KRYSTAL: It didn't work out.
PAT: Did I meet her?
KRYSTAL: We called in once—on the way to Mildura.
PAT: The one with the hair.
KRYSTAL: Yes.
PAT: Turkish?
KRYSTAL: Yes.
PAT: Don't you have any Australian friends?
KRYSTAL: They are Australians.
PAT: What about that boy you brought here?
KRYSTAL: Reza?
PAT: He was very dark.
KRYSTAL: He's Iranian. You shouted at him.
PAT: I did not.
KRYSTAL: Yes, you did. [*Shouting*] 'Do you want a cup of tea? Would you prefer coffee? Have you tried Vegemite?'
PAT: Was he a refugee?
KRYSTAL: He speaks English better than me.
PAT: How did he get here?

KRYSTAL: I think he was born here.
PAT: How did his parents get here?
KRYSTAL: It's rude to ask.
PAT: Handy.
KRYSTAL: You don't want refugees to come to Burridja. You've got a whole house you're not even using!
PAT: It's full.
KRYSTAL: Like the inn.
PAT: What?
KRYSTAL: Mary and Joseph.
PAT: You a Christian now?
KRYSTAL: Jesus was a refugee.
PAT: You are so smug. How do you stand yourself?
KRYSTAL: The Syrians are fleeing war. The Sudanese are fleeing war. Weren't the Irish fleeing something too? Wasn't there a potato famine?
PAT: In the nineteenth century.
KRYSTAL: Which makes us Irish boat people.
PAT: We didn't jump any queue.
KRYSTAL: Mum said Grandpa Tommy was more Irish than the Irish. Drank like a fish. St Patrick's Day just another excuse. Silly hats, green beer …
PAT: He missed Ireland.
KRYSTAL: Don't we have any *convict* skeletons in the cupboard?
PAT: Sorry.
KRYSTAL: At least the convicts didn't choose to invade.
PAT: Now who's feeling guilty?
KRYSTAL: *Terra nullius*, they called it. Empty land.
PAT: At last, something we can agree on.
KRYSTAL: [*pouring herself a wine*] Do you want another?
PAT: Only if it's green.

SCENE 19

Chorus—PIE, SPARRA, GOOSE.

SPARRA: Traffic.
PIE: One big queue.
GOOSE: Just get started, have to stop again.

PIE: And again.
SPARRA: And again.
GOOSE: Who'd live there?
SPARRA: The metropolis.
PIE: No chance to lift the revs.
GOOSE: Show what you got.
SPARRA: They get cranky if you push in.
PIE: Road rage.
GOOSE: Have to wait your turn.
PIE: Yous never queued to get here.
GOOSE: Some of us was born here.
PIE: What about your mum, Goose?
GOOSE: What about my mum?
PIE: She talks wog.
GOOSE: Mum's passed.
PIE: She's still talking wog—in heaven.
GOOSE: I'll sock you one.
PIE: I was born here.
GOOSE: Me too.
PIE: Your wog mum came on a boat. And your wog dad.
SPARRA: Could you stop saying wog?
PIE: Just a bit of fun.
GOOSE: Want a knuckle sandwich, Pie?
SPARRA: Let's not have an altercation.
PIE: Don't want no *al-ter-ca-shin*.
SPARRA: What're you looking at me for?
GOOSE: Only the rich can afford to pay.
SPARRA: We were ten-pound Poms. Less than twenty dollars.
GOOSE: Lot of money, them days.
PIE: Queue-jumpin' Pommy.
GOOSE: You're a boat people, Sparra.
PIE: You paid the smugglers.
SPARRA: We paid the government.
GOOSE: Your granddad come in a boat.
SPARRA: My dad, actually, Goose.
GOOSE: What about you, Pie?
PIE: Always been here, mate. Don't have to queue.

GOOSE: Bloody Abo.
PIE: Bloody wog.
GOOSE: My mum came on a ship—a liner. The *Florentia*.
PIE: Liner's still a boat, Goose.

SCENE 20

Day.

PAT *is taking photos.* KRYSTAL *appears.*

KRYSTAL: Have we got a rain gauge?
PAT: Why?
KRYSTAL: So I can talk about the weather.
PAT: It's hot.
KRYSTAL: I need specifics. I want to say, 'We had three mills at our place'.
PAT: Won't make you a country girl.
KRYSTAL: I'll be making an effort. Must be a rain gauge here somewhere.
PAT: Out by the chook pen.
KRYSTAL: How do you read it?
PAT: Never rains anyway.
KRYSTAL: I can't talk about who's related to who and who's sister-in-law's uncle had a heart attack.
PAT: That's why I stay home.
KRYSTAL: It's like your bush chorus, only with humans. People in the supermarket, outside the pub: How was your day? Joyce broke her leg. Dan ripped his toe on the barbed wire. Sorry to hear about Jason. Deb's got three now. She married Robbo's cousin. No, not Brendan. His brother, Lachie. My youngest was in his class. Doesn't she live at Woodend? We'll be up north for Christmas. See the grandkids. Give Joyce my love. Will do. Mrs Ingram hasn't got long. Sorry to hear it. I'll pop in and see her when I'm at the Village.
PAT: It's called community. Hard to find in the city.
KRYSTAL: Makes me feel like an outsider.
PAT: Maybe if you'd popped in more often.
KRYSTAL: They know where they belong. They've known the bloke serving vegetables since he was knee-high to a grasshopper.
PAT: Hardly saw you once you started school.

KRYSTAL: I brought Azra.

PAT: Just passing through.

KRYSTAL: You and Mum are as stubborn as each other.

Beat.

PAT: How's the milking?

KRYSTAL: Good.

PAT: Jim apologise?

KRYSTAL: For being a redneck?

PAT: [*pointing at the wound on her forehead*] For that.

KRYSTAL: He didn't actually hit me.

PAT: Who did?

KRYSTAL: I tried to hit him, but I was a bit drunk.

PAT: A bit.

KRYSTAL: I missed, spun around 360 degrees, hit my head on the piano.

PAT: You little drama queen.

KRYSTAL: It *looked* like he hit me. People *thought* he hit me.

PAT: Who drove you home?

KRYSTAL: Jim.

Beat.

PAT: Might need my car if I'm coming to that movie.

KRYSTAL: We could go together.

PAT: You seem to have mastered the art of driving short distances.

KRYSTAL: I'm making an effort.

PAT: You can be the designated driver.

KRYSTAL: What makes you think there'll be grog?

PAT: Aren't you on the committee?

SCENE 21

Night.

PAT *and* RAFFAELE *on the verandah.* PAT *has a glass of wine.*

RAFFAELE: When we come here in Australia they throw rotten eggs and *pomodori*, tomato. They call us *l'oglio*. The garlic. They call us Italian chicken, but everyone is scared in war. They call us wog bastard. I think, 'What is this hell place?' I think, 'Why, God, did you bring us to this hell land?'

I work on orchard farm. Pick *la frutta: arance, mele, limone*. All day till my arm on fire like when I break in my village. We sing when we pick fruit.

They carry us to work in truck. We sing in truck. *Così*.

He sings in Italian.

We live in forest—in camp. We play music. We have books. *Inglese* books. I practise English. Gianni make *il giardino*, grow tomatoes. *Basilica*. Make *salsa di pomodoro* like Mamma—smell like home: *basilica, oglio, cipolle, origano*. I make *animali australiani*. Use little knife—with wood from forest.

One day Bluey stop outside pub and we wait in truck, singing *Italiano*.

He sings.

Man come and say stop singing so loud so bloody wog. Speak the lingo. He say police arrest us for making public nuisance. So many things to be arrested. Must not smoke on parade. Seven day detention. One shilling for wasting water. Three days for pretend sick. *Vent'otto*, twenty-eight days detention for 'unduly familiar with female'. Bluey say must not talk to the woman.

PAT: What am I, chopped liver?

SCENE 22

Day.

The sound of hammering.

PAT *is drinking coffee.* KRYSTAL *emerges.*

PAT: What was all that banging?
KRYSTAL: Just making my bed.
PAT: With a hammer?
KRYSTAL: I was fixing something.
PAT: What?
KRYSTAL: [*indicating the coffee pot*] Is that fresh?
PAT: Fresh enough.

    KRYSTAL *pours coffee.*

KRYSTAL: Look what I found.

KRYSTAL *produces little emu carvings.*

PAT: [*furious, snatching at them*] Give them to me. Stay out of my house.

KRYSTAL: They're so cute. Are they Aboriginal?

> PAT *snatches them from* KRYSTAL*'s hands. They fall to the ground.* PAT *falls to the floor, scrabbling to pick them up.* KRYSTAL *tries to help.*

PAT: Get away. Don't touch. Look what you've done.

KRYSTAL: It's not broken.

PAT: It's scratched.

KRYSTAL: What's wrong with you?

PAT: What right have you to invade my home?

KRYSTAL: House full of junk.

PAT: [*polishing a carving*] I didn't invite you here. Get out. Go on. I don't want you here.

KRYSTAL: I'm going. Don't worry.

PAT: Go then. Go on. Get out. Get. How dare you?

KRYSTAL: I'll never come back. I'll leave you here talking to your stupid house. You crazy old lady. Crazy old lady hoarder. Mum always said you were weird.

PAT: She knows nothing.

KRYSTAL: She said you've got worse since Grandpa died.

PAT: That's how much she doesn't know.

KRYSTAL: She doesn't know the half of it.

PAT: I've never been better.

KRYSTAL: You're deluded.

PAT: Where is your mother anyway?

KRYSTAL: What's that got to do with it?

PAT: She never visits.

KRYSTAL: I wonder why?

PAT: Thought you were off.

KRYSTAL: She's off finding herself. Having adventures.

PAT: Plenty of adventures to have here in Burridja.

KRYSTAL: Why don't you want me in Burridja having adventures?

PAT: You're a sticky beak, that's why. You have no respect.

KRYSTAL: You're just like Grandma.

PAT: I'm nothing like my mother. She was tall.

KRYSTAL: She was mean.
PAT: She was tidy.
KRYSTAL: Mean and uptight.
PAT: Am I? Mean and uptight?
KRYSTAL: Not all the time.
PAT: I don't mean to be mean.
KRYSTAL: I didn't mean to take your stupid birds.
PAT: You went into my room. Is that where you're sleeping?
KRYSTAL: You never go in there. Why do you care?
PAT: They were Lily's.
KRYSTAL: The emus?
PAT: Dad made me a special shelf.
KRYSTAL: I didn't know.
PAT: I lined them up, watching me in bed. I used to talk to them.
KRYSTAL: [*arranging them on the verandah*] They can watch you out here.
PAT: It's not the same.
KRYSTAL: Sorry, Grummy.

> *Beat.*

Mum's in Italy.
PAT: You've heard from her?
KRYSTAL: Of course.

SCENE 23

Chorus—PIE, SPARRA, GOOSE.

PIE: [*to* GOOSE] Your dad doesn't even speak the lingo.
GOOSE: Does too.
PIE: Couple of words Aussie—the rest all wog.
SPARRA: His dad speaks five languages.
GOOSE: You only speak la-dee-dah.
PIE: 'To who-oom.'
SPARRA: I'm on your side, Goose.
PIE: Your dad speaks wog. You speak wog.
GOOSE: You're a bastard. That English enough for you? You're a bastard and your mother's a lady dog.
SPARRA: You'd both fail the dictation test.

GOOSE: [*to* PIE] Your dad's still drawing dots in the dirt.
PIE: Your dad come in a boat. You're a boat people. Turn back the boats! Should of turned you back two hundred years ago.
SPARRA: Makes you think.
PIE: Your dad drowned his kids. Your wog dad. Threw 'em overboard.
GOOSE: I'm right here—alive and kicking.
PIE: His other kids.
SPARRA: Wog's not such a bad word these days. It's been reclaimed.
GOOSE: If I'm a wog, you're a poofter. Reclaim that, you bastard.
SPARRA: Watch it.
GOOSE: Your dad's a poofter too.
PIE: You can get married now.
SPARRA: Not to my dad I can't.
GOOSE: So you admit you're a poofter.
PIE: Hold your place. Quick. He's coming.
GOOSE: Who?
PIE: It's B.J.

They squash up close.

GOOSE: Wait your fucking turn, mate.

SCENE 24

Day.

PAT *is photographing birds.* KRYSTAL *sits.*

KRYSTAL: You know that old guy who sits in front of the pub?
PAT: Which old guy?
KRYSTAL: Jim said, 'He might have a touch of the tar brush'.
PAT: Oh, that old guy.
KRYSTAL: Couldn't get away with it in the city.
PAT: You're not in the city.
KRYSTAL: It's offensive. Hurtful.
PAT: Agreed.
KRYSTAL: What?
PAT: That stopped you in your tracks, didn't it?
KRYSTAL: There are laws.
PAT: Racial Discrimination Act, passed 1975.
KRYSTAL: Burridja's like a backwater.

PAT: No point trying to reinvent the wheel.

KRYSTAL: It's time you oldies listened to young people.

PAT: Says the girl going on forty.

KRYSTAL: You old people have fucked up the world, now it's our turn. We're not going to take racism—or sexual harassment, wage theft, narrow-minded, binary thinking—

PAT: You might like to pick your battles. You can't actually expect to win. You can't change people.

KRYSTAL: You've changed.

PAT: Don't bring me into it.

KRYSTAL: You didn't always live on a verandah.

PAT: I moved out here off my own bat. I changed myself.

KRYSTAL: Are you ready to go?

PAT: Where?

KRYSTAL: To the movie?

PAT: What movie?

KRYSTAL: You said you'd come.

PAT: Dunno what you're—?

KRYSTAL: It's about a woman in Tasmania who knits beanies for refugees. She hates Muslims, but then she meets Mohammad. I think a couple of the Afghan refugees from Swan Hill are coming.

PAT: I'll make you a deal.

KRYSTAL: Okay.

PAT: I'll come if …

KRYSTAL: What?

PAT: … you come for a walk in the forest. Look at the red gums, listen to the birds.

KRYSTAL: Will I have to smell any wattle?

PAT: I'll show you where Aboriginal people used to live. We might find some clay balls. See an emu.

KRYSTAL: Will you let me clear out the back room?

PAT: Don't push it.

SCENE 25

Night.

PAT *and* RAFFAELE. *The sound of a kookaburra laughing. A magpie.*

RAFFAELE: Bird laughs at my red *pantaloni*.
PAT: She just wants meat.
RAFFAELE: You give meat? *Carne?*
PAT: Just a bit of mince. Maggies like it too.
RAFFAELE: He is very happy bird. *Molto contento*.
PAT: How do you know he's a he?
RAFFAELE: All birds are man in my language. *L'uccello*. Today I see eem-you, Patrizia.
PAT: Emu?
RAFFAELE: *Sì. Sono contento.*
PAT: Where?
RAFFAELE: In forest. *Molto grande*. Bird with roof like African house.
PAT: That roof is made of feathers.
RAFFAELE: *Mi piace cosi tanto*. I watch it run. I am running too. Bird is *molto veloce*. Very fast. We run *insieme*. Together.
PAT: It can't fly, you know.
RAFFAELE: But can run.
PAT: Fast as a car.

SCENE 26

Night.

KRYSTAL *and* JIM *are having a drink.*

JIM: You did well today.
KRYSTAL: Thanks. I tried not to let the cows pick up my stress.
JIM: Don't want to spook them.
KRYSTAL: I didn't expect so much … poo.
JIM: Told you. Old clothes.
KRYSTAL: It's so earthy. So intimate. Standing in the pit, all those bursting udders staring you in the face. I'm in love with that black cow with the long eyelashes.
JIM: Oh, *that* one.
KRYSTAL: You know her?
JIM: That's half the Friesian herd.
KRYSTAL: She's got a white triangle just above her nose. She likes to be scratched.
JIM: Probably Chanel. She loves attention.

KRYSTAL: They're so big. So sensitive.
JIM: Too sensitive.
KRYSTAL: You didn't tell me they had names.
JIM: Chanel, Coco, Charlie, Joy, Opium …
KRYSTAL: Perfumes.
JIM: One year it was jewels: Ruby, Topaz, Opal, Diamond, Amber, Pearl, Jade … Jade's that stubborn little Jersey. The newest arrivals are just ordinary old Cindy, Sue and Kate.
KRYSTAL: How do you remember them all?
JIM: I love my cows. Even more now I'm on me own. Gives me something to get up for. My wife's been gone three years.
KRYSTAL: Sorry.
JIM: I'm doing okay. I can't cook. I'm eating dog food. Dog looks up, can I have some of that? Things are better since I got voted mayor. Now I'm too busy to think. Sometimes I get lucky and they feed me.

Beat.

Think you can handle the work then?
KRYSTAL: [*nodding*] I like the washout. Standing there with that pressure hose, watching all the shit go flying—makes everything fresh and new.
JIM: Got to do it all again in a few hours.
KRYSTAL: Do you like being a dairy farmer?
JIM: Grew up on a farm.
KRYSTAL: But do you like it?
JIM: [*nodding*] When we first got married, thirty odd years ago, we had a little old flat shed. The cows would just walk to each bale and you'd squat down, put the cups on—right beside the cow.
KRYSTAL: Don't you get sick of getting up at five in the morning?
JIM: That's what *you're* for—so I can have the odd sleep-in.
KRYSTAL: So much to remember.
JIM: You'll get there.

Beat.

KRYSTAL: Grummy took me into the forest yesterday.
JIM: [*impressed*] Pat left the house?
KRYSTAL: The Aborigines had whole villages—with fish ponds and gardens.

JIM: I know.
KRYSTAL: We saw all these middens. They were covered in Patterson's curse, like purple cushions.
JIM: I know.
KRYSTAL: She showed me a scarred tree. They cut out the bark to make a canoe.
JIM: I know.
KRYSTAL: I found a clay ball.

She digs it from her pocket.

The children roll up balls of clay—you can still see their little fingerprints—to use in the oven instead of rocks. Those fingerprints are hundreds of years old. Did you know there are no rocks in Burridja? None!

JIM *nods.*

All those children taken away from their families. Imagine being chucked in a mission? Told your mother's dead.
JIM: You moving onto a new cause?
KRYSTAL: How could you ever be a good parent?
JIM: You don't even live here.
KRYSTAL: Yes, I do. I've even got a job.
JIM: You're a blow-in.
KRYSTAL: Maybe you need an outsider's perspective.
JIM: Half the time I don't even know what you're talking about. You get so fired up.
KRYSTAL: Why don't you?
JIM: What?
KRYSTAL: Get fired up.
JIM: I get fired up. It just doesn't pour out my mouth. I'm fired up about them dropping the price on our milk. I wake up every morning—someone's screaming, 'Bastards!' It's me—yelling into my pillow. What a low act. Charging us back pay too. There used to be dairy farms everywhere. Now it's just crumbling old schools, box thorns and dillon bush.
KRYSTAL: Do something. You're the mayor.
JIM: I'm working on it. But the cows have to be milked.
KRYSTAL: By me.

JIM: Come a bit earlier tomorrow. You can bring them in from the paddock and set the gates for the home run.

SCENE 27

Night.

PAT *and* RAFFAELE *sit beside each other on the verandah.* PAT *has a glass of wine.*

RAFFAELE: At home I drink only *vino* and never *troppo*, never drunk, but in Australia I must be a man. No tears.
PAT: Only beers.
RAFFAELE: *Troppo caldo*. Too hot. I hate this suit. They make from old army uniform then they make red. I am red like lobster boiling in the sun. Red like target. Boss say so we cannot run away.
  Only boobook owl hear me cry in my bed. [*He makes the sound.*] Boo-book. Boo-book.

SCENE 28

Day.

KRYSTAL *flicks through images on her phone. She laughs.*

PAT *peeks over* KRYSTAL*'s shoulder.*

KRYSTAL: Classic selfie.
PAT: Alison and the Eiffel Tower. What a cliché.
KRYSTAL: She's deconstructing.
PAT: Speak English.
KRYSTAL: Unpicking the stereotype of the tourist.
PAT: Why would she do that?
KRYSTAL: To make me laugh.
PAT: Funny sense of humour.
KRYSTAL: You never tried to understand.
PAT: That you talking—or your mother?
KRYSTAL: Both.
PAT: I didn't have the luxury of a good education. Mum said it was wasted on girls. I made sure Alison got to uni.
KRYSTAL: *Elena.*
PAT: Who?

KRYSTAL: I keep telling you. She's *Elena* now.

Her phone goes off—a tooting train. She reads a text. She cheers.

O. M. G! Oh my God. Grummy! It's Renee. Listen to this. [*Reading aloud*] 'Second time lucky. We are now officially a Refugee Welcome Zone. They added one word: "Refugee and *Migrant* Friendly Zone". We did it.' [*She looks up.*] Can you believe that? The motion's been passed.

PAT: Suppose you'll be off soon then.

KRYSTAL: Stop that.

PAT: Stop what?

KRYSTAL: Stop pretending you don't care.

PAT: Haven't you finished what you came for?

KRYSTAL: 'Refugee and *Migrant* Friendly Zone'. That's good. We're all migrants.

PAT: Except our First People.

Beat.

KRYSTAL: We need to have a talk.

PAT: Why?

KRYSTAL: You better sit down, Grummy.

PAT: I'll sit when I'm ready.

KRYSTAL: Mum's in Italy.

PAT: Holding up the Tower of Pisa.

KRYSTAL: She's done her DNA and she's found out stuff—about our family.

PAT: What stuff?

KRYSTAL: Big stuff. She's going to ring you tonight, but she said I can [*making speech marks in the air*] 'prepare you for the call'.

PAT: [*the Irish in her*] Jesus, Mary and Joseph.

KRYSTAL: Mum says we're Italian. That's why she changed her name. She's gone all *Italiano*.

PAT: Don't be ridiculous.

KRYSTAL: She's a quarter Italian, which means I'm an eighth.

PAT: Alison was never satisfied with reality.

KRYSTAL: It's true, Grummy. DNA doesn't lie. Mum's found a whole lot of second cousins over there.

PAT: That's impossible.

KRYSTAL: Great Aunt Lily has been there too.

    PAT *sits.*

PAT: Lily?

KRYSTAL: Mum said they had photos from when Lily visited in the sixties. Lily told them she had a relationship with one of the Italian prisoners of war.

PAT: Lily?

KRYSTAL: And she confided in one of her Italian cousins that she had a baby.

PAT: What?

KRYSTAL: Lily had a baby, Grummy. When she was still in Burridja.

PAT: A baby?

KRYSTAL: We think that baby was you, Grummy. The time frame fits. Explains why she disappeared. Grandma Eileen must have thought Lily was too young to have a baby. Eileen was your grandma, Grummy.

PAT: Lily?

KRYSTAL: Are you okay? It's a lot to take in. We could try to ring Mum.

    PAT *picks up one of the emu carvings.*

PAT: She always sent a card on my birthday. Eileen said I was better off without her.

KRYSTAL: You're half Italian.

PAT: I can't be.

KRYSTAL: A wog.

PAT: Italian?

KRYSTAL: Lily's boyfriend had an accident and died here, in Burridja. There were a whole lot of prisoners standing in the back of a truck.

PAT: I wonder how many people in town knew?

KRYSTAL: Two men died.

PAT: I bet everyone knows.

KRYSTAL: There's a gravestone in the cemetery.

PAT: What were their names? The men who died.

KRYSTAL: [*consulting her phone*] Gianni d'Alberto and Raffaele Contadino.

PAT: Raffaele? Raff?

KRYSTAL: Isn't that what you call your house?

PAT: How could I be Italian?

KRYSTAL: You make excellent coffee. Culture filters down. Like coffee.

PAT: Lily?

KRYSTAL: Lily died in London in 2005. She was eighty-one. I'm sorry, Grummy.

PAT: One Christmas she sent a pair of jeans, but they were too small.

> KRYSTAL *hugs* PAT.

SCENE 29

Night.

RAFFAELE *is talking.* PAT *sits at his feet, like a child.*

RAFFAELE: We work hard all day on Tommy's farm. Tommy scream like cockatoo. He comes back from war with crook leg. Call us 'sissy boy' and 'bastard'. He say, 'You too weak to win war, bloody wogs, son of Mussolini. Too limp to lift chainsaw let alone fight, bloody dago mummy-boy wog.'

Every time Tommy the boss speak, I think is normal. He say get in the fucking truck. Get me the fucking ladder. Hurry the fuck up. This is a fucking great cuppa. So one day he say you go and get the tea and I say okay. The boss's daughter was in the kitchen window, doing cleaning. She smile at me. I say, 'Miss, we want the fucking tea, and some fucking biscuits, *per favore*'. The girl is laughing. The boss's wife Eileen run out the door and call back to Tommy, 'Why you teach them this?' Tommy come to me and said, 'Raff, you no say these words to the ladies. That's very bad.' So I went to the ladies and say sorry. I didn't mean it. The girl say, no worries. Not your fault. My name is Lily, what's yours? That's how I met Lily. I say to her, my name is Raffaele.

Lily is *bella*. She is daughter to Eileen. She work at farm too. *Alla fattoria.* Help Eileen in kitchen. Clean house. Pick fruit. Everyone like Lily, she smile and laugh. Help pick up oranges. She says, *'Ciao. Raffaele'* and her eyes are like *stelle*. Like Milky Way. Lily touch my hand on the ladder. *Lily è bella.*

SCENE 30

Day.

JIM *and* KRYSTAL *are on the verandah, drinking.*

JIM: Reconciliation Week gets bigger every year.
KRYSTAL: Thought there were only two Aborigines in Burridja.
JIM: Lucky for us one of them plays didgeridoo.
KRYSTAL: Where did they all come from?
JIM: Farms, other towns. Lots of supportive whities this year. Where's Pat?
KRYSTAL: She left early this morning. Took the car. And her binoculars.
JIM: Birdwatching.
KRYSTAL: She got jealous 'cause I saw a flotilla of pelicans at Henty Swamp. She hasn't driven that car for ages.
JIM: We were expecting her at the march.
KRYSTAL: Grummy never goes anywhere. She hates people. [*Quoting*] She's with the birds.
JIM: None of this would've happened without Pat, you know.
KRYSTAL: None of what?
JIM: The Reconciliation March. The smoking ceremony. The Aboriginal flag in the main street. Don't you know anything about your own grandma?
KRYSTAL: You'd be surprised.
JIM: She used to be mayor.
KRYSTAL: Shut up.
JIM: Few years back.
KRYSTAL: Mayor?
JIM: She wanted us to acknowledge the traditional owners—have a Welcome to Country. We were arguing about it for years. Pat was nearly thrown out of council chambers. But she stood up to us. Kept chipping away until she got that flag up.

Re-enactment:

PAT: *Formal events should begin with an acknowledgment of the traditional owners. Or a welcome from a member of the local Indigenous community. Every day we live with privilege, we're oppressing someone. We're all responsible one hundred percent. If we don't do anything to change anything ...*
KRYSTAL: [*confused*] Grummy hates change.
JIM: She put up with a lot.
SPARRA: *Load of rubbish.*
GOOSE: *Tokenism.*

SPARRA: *Don't welcome me to my own bloody country.*
GOOSE: *Just a way to tell ordinary Australians that they don't belong here.*
SPARRA: *Not even a part of Aboriginal culture.*
GOOSE: *I heard some actors invented that Welcome thing back in the seventies.*
SPARRA: *How much does this little ceremony cost—for ten minutes work? They're laughing all the way to the bank.*
GOOSE: *I'm not going to pay some clown to read a prepared speech to thank the local whatsit tribe.*
SPARRA: *The Whatever Tribe of Wherever—for allowing us to use our own land.*
GOOSE: *You know what it's really about?*
SPARRA: *They're after our land.*
GOOSE: *They're not getting my land. I bought my property outright.*
PAT: *Given two hundred years of denial, it's a small gesture of respect. Only a couple of Aborigines living in town anyway. How scared are you? The rest moved away because you make 'em uncomfortable. Most were massacred two centuries ago—by colonials, like us. We brought colds, measles, typhoid ... There used to be hundreds of Indigenous people living in the forest. Settlers poisoned them, shot them, sent them off to Coranderrk and Cummeragunja reserves. It's not about who owns what.*
KRYSTAL: Grummy said that?
PAT: *Why is it so threatening to acknowledge the past?*
JIM: Kept it up for years. We didn't give her an easy time of it.
PAT: *[to the audience] I didn't think sexism was real till I got into Council. Even when I was new, some of the older men ignored me. Wouldn't talk to a woman. They don't think you've got a brain. I had a code. I wasn't going to yell and I wasn't going to cry and I wasn't going to hang up on anyone.*
JIM: It took it out of her. No wonder she's hiding out here in the forest. But she won in the end. All good things come to those who nag.
KRYSTAL: That's my plan.
JIM: You're a lot like your grandmother.
KRYSTAL: I hope so.

    Beat.

JIM: We're going to make Harmony Day bigger next year. It's about inclusiveness, respect and belonging for all Australians regardless of cultural background.

KRYSTAL: Listen to Mr I've-Seen-*When-Mary-Meets-Mohammad*.

JIM: It wasn't just the film. It was meeting Rahoola and Raji. At first I thought Rahoola looked a bit suss. I wasn't sure how to take him—whether he was happy to see me or he was planning something.

KRYSTAL: Like what?

JIM: I couldn't even pronounce Rahoola at first. Kept saying 'Ruler'. Rahoola saw all his family shot and slaughtered. On TV, you think that's nothing to do with us, but this man shook my hand.

He shows the movement.

They go to the head, to the heart, and out to the side, all with the right hand. That's their greeting to you. Everyone was just running, falling … People were shot down in front of him. He couldn't stop to save his family. [*He chokes.*] Then Raji taught me how to say all the fruit in his language: watermelon is *tar-booz*.

KRYSTAL: In Afghan?

JIM: In Dari. It's like Afghan Persian.

KRYSTAL: [*impressed*] Is it?

JIM: We're a welcoming community.

KRYSTAL: Now.

JIM: A Refugee Friendly Zone.

KRYSTAL: In spirit.

JIM: Gotta start somewhere.

SCENE 31

Chorus—PIE, SPARRA, GOOSE.

PIE: What're they all queuing up for?
GOOSE: Dunno.
SPARRA: Haven't you heard?
PIE: What?
SPARRA: Everyone's going to the top garage.
GOOSE: What for?
SPARRA: They're selling curry. Takeaway Indian.

GOOSE: Yeah?
SPARRA: Started last Sunday.
PIE: Any good?
SPARRA: They'd sold out by seven.
GOOSE: Better get a move on then.
PIE: See ya.
SPARRA: Tomorrow?
PIE: At Chinese Trev's.
SPARRA: Who's Trev?
PIE: Jesus.
SPARRA: Trev's not a very Chinese name.
GOOSE: Used to be Trevor Kelly's Takeaway.
SPARRA: Oh.
PIE: The penny drops.
GOOSE: Know where you're going?
SPARRA: Think so. See you.
GOOSE: Not if I see you first.
PIE: One main street.
GOOSE: Sparra still gets lost.

SCENE 32

RAFFAELE *and* PAT *stand in front of the stage, a distance between them. They speak in blended monologue.*

PAT: A pelican hangs low over the road. Chest puffed. Pink beak sharp as an arrow.
RAFFAELE: Bluey is boss at camp in forest. He not so bad. Not like Tommy.
PAT: A dinosaur in the sky.
RAFFAELE: Noworriesmate, he say.
PAT: Heavy as a plane; light as a balloon.
RAFFAELE: Noworriesmate.
PAT: The pelican floats just above my windscreen.
RAFFAELE: Bluey drive us to work at farm. We stand in back.
PAT: With a twitch of black wing, the bird tilts.
RAFFAELE: Many men squash in truck.
PAT: Buoyant as a surfboard.

RAFFAELE: After work, we singing, laughing, shouting.
PAT: My car slips under its snowy belly.
RAFFAELE: We go back to camp, chop wood, light fire, sing. Go bed. Cry for Mamma.
PAT: Time slows.
RAFFAELE: Get up. Bluey drive us to work.
PAT: I search for my camera.
RAFFAELE: *Sempre la stessa.* Always the same.
PAT: I forget to drive.
RAFFAELE: One night, Bluey come late to farm. The sky is *arancione*, then sun gone. We are hungry, thinking of dinner.
PAT: The pelican follows the creek, eye on the water.
RAFFAELE: Bluey say hurry hurry. Gotta go.
PAT: I follow the track, heading west.
RAFFAELE: Get in truck, mate. Come on, I got hot date, he say.
PAT: I duck my head. Sense its warmth graze the roof.
RAFFAELE: Bluey is laughing.
PAT: Millimetres from blood and feathers.
RAFFAELE: I am singing.
PAT: I drift to the left, catch the steering wheel with my elbow.
RAFFAELE: Suddenly eem-you is on truck.
PAT: The car has a mind of its own.
RAFFAELE: *Collisione!*
PAT: My foot stiffens on the brake. The wheels spin.
RAFFAELE: Truck jump in field. Truck upside down.
PAT: I hear a cat wailing, glass breaking.
RAFFAELE: I hear smack in my head.
PAT: I hear tyres squealing.
RAFFAELE: I hear screaming.
PAT: I see leaves, twigs, a fence post.
RAFFAELE: *Aiuto!*
PAT: Smell petrol.
RAFFAELE: I hear *mio amico: Aiuto!* Help!
PAT: A flash of blue sky, a crack of lightning.
RAFFAELE: My friend Gianni shouting.
PAT: A rush of brown water.
RAFFAELE: Raffaele!

PAT: I hear an emu booming. It must be close.
RAFFAELE: **Raffaele!**
PAT: I run to see.

THE END

presents

RUNNING WITH EMUS

by
Merrilee Moss

11-22 March 2020

PATRICIA REILLY **Julie Nihill**
KRYSTAL / RENEE **Elizabeth Sly**
RAFFAELE / GOOSE **Sam Baxter**
JIM / SPARRA **Kevin Dee**
PIE **Gregory J Fryer**

Director **Kim Durban**
Designer **Adam (Gus) Powers**
Cover image **Darren Gill**

CEO & Artistic Director
Liz Jones

CEO and Manager / Producer
Caitlin Dullard

Venue Manager
Hayley Fox

Front-of-House Manager
Amber Hart

Marketing and Communications
Sophia Constantine

Social Media
Solange Parraguez

Learning Producer and School Publications Coordinator
Maureen Hartley

Preservation Coordinator
Fiona Wiseman

Office Co-ordinator
Elena Larkin

Curators
Gemma Horbury (Musica); **Amanda Anastasi** (Poetica);
Susan Bamford-Caleo and **Isabel Knight** (Cabaretica)

La Mama office is currently at:
La Mama Courthouse, 349 Drummond Street, Carlton, Vic 3053
www.lamama.com.au | info@lamama.com.au
facebook.com/lamama.theatre | twitter.com/lamamatheatre
Office phone 03 9347 6948 | Office Mon–Fri, 10:30am–5:30pm;
weekends 1pm–3PM.

FRONT OF HOUSE STAFF

Amber Hart, Maureen Hartley, Caitlin Dullard, Elena Larkin, Solange Parraguez, Sophia Constantine, Laurence Strangio, Carmelina Di Guglielmo, Hayley Fox, Susan Bamford-Caleo, Dennis Coard, Isabel Knight, Dora Abraham, Zac Kazepis, and Phil Roberts.

COMMITTEE OF MANAGEMENT

Richard Watts, Dur-é Dara, Ben Grant, Caitlin Dullard, Caroline Lee, David Levin, Helen Hopkins, Sue Broadway, Beng Oh and Liz Jones.

La Mama Theatre is on traditional land. We pay our respect to all First Nations people, past and present, and we recognise their continuing spiritual and cultural connection to the land.

La Mama is financially assisted by the Australian Government through the Australia Council – its arts funding and advisory body, the Victorian Government through Creative Victoria, and the City of Melbourne through the Arts and Culture Triennial Funding Program.

We are grateful to all our philanthropic partners and donors, advocates, volunteers, audiences, artists and our entire community as we work towards the La Mama rebuild. Thank you!

.

WRITER'S NOTE

The inspiration for *Running With Emus* came when I moved from Melbourne to the small town of Cohuna in 2014. Despite many welcoming gestures from the community, I felt an unexpected and uncomfortable level of culture shock. As a 'newcomer' or 'blow-in', I was cast into the role of outsider. But on the plus side, this provided a unique point of view and I began to enjoy collecting snippets of dialogue, noting similarities and differences, jotting down descriptions, observing opinions and habits. It seemed strange to me, for example, that people drove everywhere when the town was not much bigger than a shopping mall. When it rained, no-one used an umbrella, they just rushed about looking up at the sky with a puzzled expression. I began a column in the town's newsletter called 'Notes from a Newcomer' where I pondered these things. About the same time, I accompanied the Gannawarra Refugee Support group to a Shire meeting where it put a motion to make the Shire a 'Refugee Friendly Zone'. These two things combined to kick-start my creative journey.

On a broader level, I was inspired and impressed with the generosity and vision shown by communities of 'dying' Australian towns such as Mingoola NSW, and Nhill Victoria, which took in refugees and, by doing so, reinvigorated their own economies and communities. This is a worldwide phenomenon. Riace, Italy, for example, has welcomed more than 6,000 migrants since 1998. Their town used to have high unemployment and an ageing population (like Cohuna), but was revived by an influx of refugees who brought their own culture and knowledge.

I used these issues to infuse the story, characters and conflicts represented in *Running with Emus*. The play is inspired by, and in conversation with, the local dynamics of Cohuna, while it attempts to mirror all sides of the important global debate, including universal themes such as belonging and identity, as represented in the microcosm of a small community.

I continue to enjoy the quiet of Cohuna, the birds, the local humour, the sparkling sky at night. I have learned to drive short distances and I rarely carry an umbrella.—**Merrilee Moss**

DIRECTOR'S NOTE

It is an exciting proposition to premiere a new play because, not only has nobody ever seen it, nobody has ever heard it, and nobody has ever said it aloud (except perhaps the writer muttering in her study). Consequently, the look, the sound and the taste of a new play are always, for me, delicious. In *Running With Emus*, there is a litany of Aussie ideas in the chorus of dissent running through the plot that I recognise, and I am attracted to the centrality of a mature woman at the heart of this play. Pat is a marvellous creature and her stubbornness grounds the story.

Because *Running With Emus* appears to be about the real world, the premiere season in Cohuna was packed with real objects arrayed on a definitively real verandah in the open air.

But, just as theatre is always a composed version of real life, so the play poeticises this environment. Some scenes occur at night, that time of dreams and doubts and desires, butted up against scenes that are raucous with attitude, written to be played unashamedly in full daylight.

The play champions female independence and experience in the face of the world's dismissal. Counterpointed by bird song and surrounded by the bush, the voices of the actors in *Emus* are from different places, ages and backgrounds. This is deliberate and this is a reflection of Merrilee Moss's Australia.

In writing this note, it is hard to avoid the production's link to place and space. We are mounting the production at a time when our country is burning and people are looking for hope. *Running With Emus*, with its dry humour and cross-generational embrace, gives those flashes of hope some room, celebrating the wisdom of the old, the reflections of the country and the feisty energy of the young as they work to create a refuge that can change their world.—**Kim Durban**

DESIGNER'S NOTE

Having grown up in the Mallee, *Running With Emus* has, for me, a visual landscape that feels very much like 'home'. The colour of the earth, the smell of the hot red gums and that all-embracing sky is incredibly familiar and a landscape in which I first dreamt, especially on the long car trips of my childhood. It is such a wonderful treat to visually approach a new work, and one set in the playground of my childhood is infinitely rare.

Premiering in Cohuna at Treetops provided us with the **setting**, the house, the physical landscape in which we played. To tell Merrilee Moss's story however required smaller design details upon the verandah of that house—the world of Pat. How does someone live on their verandah? How do you survive the heat of summer, the dust, the cold and the rain? And how does this world also include the landscape of Pat's dreaming?

Given this production opened in Cohuna and then moved inside to a theatre in Carlton, the world we created needed to be transferable, so all the scenic elements needed to reflect the objects we couldn't transfer—the house and verandah, the sky, the timber and trees, the birds. The **costumes** had to belong in this landscape, with consideration of how the characters of the play live their lives, representing their past, their present and their aspirations.

The **minimal props** reflected the world of the play, but they also needed to be practical and, given the intimate nature of their physical relationship with the performer, appropriate and realistic.—**Adam (Gus) Powers**

APPROACH TO PERFORMANCE STYLE

Running with Emus uses a diverse and cross-generational cast. On the surface, the play appears to be realistic, but it is also metatheatrical in its more playful scenes and uses a chorus of laconic locals to comment on its processes and themes.

The chorus in *Running with Emus* adds an element of non-naturalism to the play: on one level it is pure entertainment, apparently disconnected from the main action, but on a deeper level, under the guise of humour, it asks the spectator to reflect on and critique their own attitudes to the 'newcomer', and to question their identity in the context of colonialism and current global events.

A character in the play, Raffaele, symbolises the remnants of the migrant experience in a regional town, the loss of connection experienced by the newcomer, and brings a hint of cultural diversity from another era.

While the setting of the drama rarely strays from a cluttered farm verandah (with a nod to traditional Australian classics such as *The*

Drover's Wife), dramatic elements occur that take us elsewhere: character transformations, transitions of time, a ghostly presence and a gradual exposition of the play's secrets to build dramatic tension, conflict and rhythm. The main protagonist Patricia engages with the audience via monologue, breaking the fourth wall.

The central image comes from the native birds of the local red gum forest. The title of the play, *Running with Emus*, is also a metaphor for what it is to truly live and belong in Australia.

LIGHTING DESIGN

The lighting supports and enriches the natural elements of the play's setting, the red for the earth, the grey-green for the bush and the blue for the sky. Night and Day are obvious locations: Morning takes us to a more tenderly lit environment and the ghost of Raff and the chorus live both in time and outside of time, leading to a dream-like intensity.

SOUND DESIGN

A soundscape of Australian birdsong, popular music and contemporary songs, used in this production, mirrors the interests of the characters.

WRITER'S ACKNOWLEDGEMENTS

I would like to thank many people and organisations for their generous support during the creation and production of *Emus*. Specific individuals I need to mention are: Kim Bennett, Lorraine Learmouth (the Mayor), Margot and Stephen Henty, Ken and Glenda Adams, Judy and John Worrall, Jacqueline Hibbert, Tucker Peace, the members of the Gannawarra Refugee Support Group, Cathy and Pete Donehue, Kirsty Orr, Dianne Upton and Jodie Hay.

My research was supported by a grant from the Australia Council, and Regional Arts Victoria funded the World Premiere launch event held at the Tree Tops Scout Camp on the edge of the Gannawarra forest (Feb, 2020). The project has also been supported by Federation University, the Shire of Gannawarra, the Cohuna Historical Society, the Cohuna Neighbourhood House, the Cohuna Lions Club and the Waters Edge Walking Group.

I am beyond grateful to La Mama Theatre, and particularly thank

Liz Jones and Maureen Hartley, who have nurtured my art for decades and now accepted my tenth script into their 2020 season.

I would like to thank Tanya Black for helping with the day-to-day organisation in Cohuna and for believing that anything is possible. Bookings for the launch at Tree Tops Scout Camp blew out all expectations (unusual in a traditionally sports-centric community) and more and more Cohuna volunteers emerged to direct traffic, run front-of-house, find chairs, cater, serve drinks and solve problems never before faced by a playwright from the city.

I would like to thank all the Cohuna volunteers, particularly Elaine Keely, Rhonda Ballard, Marion Smith, Ros Dwyer, Denise Morrison, Des and Marie Hudson, Lee and Norm Walkington.

And finally, a huge thank you to the three people who read the script in its early phases and provided me with essential critical feedback: Annette Blonski, Meg Mappin and Helen Edwards.—**Merrilee Moss**

MERRILEE (MOSS) MOSS
PLAYWRIGHT

KIM DURBAN
DIRECTOR

Moss is an award-winning Victorian playwright. Her nine plays include *If Looks Could Kill* (1988), *Over the Hill* (1989), *Empty Suitcases* (1993) and *Tango Femme* (2011). In 2010, her play *Night Breakfast* won the Community and Youth Australian Writers Guild Industry Excellence (AWGIE) Award. In 2014 her play *Oriel* was awarded a High Commendation in the R.E. Ross Playwrights' Development Awards. *Oriel* had a season at La Mama Courthouse Theatre in 2016. Moss has a PhD in Theatre Performance from Monash University. She has also published novels, including the adventure series for young adults *Hot Pursuit* and a novel for 7-11 year olds, *Thriller & Me*.

Kim Durban initially trained as a teacher in South Australia, then as a director at the Victorian College of the Arts. Over her career she has built a strong reputation as a director of both new plays and classic texts for theatres across Australia, including Melbourne Theatre Company, State Theatre of South Australia, Queensland Theatre Company, Playbox Theatre, La Mama Theatre and Red Stitch Actors' Theatre. Her production of *Oriel* by Merrilee Moss was seen at the Carlton Courthouse in 2016. In 2001, Kim was appointed Senior Lecturer in Performing Arts at Federation University in Ballarat, where significant productions include *Margaret of Anjou, As You Like It, Machinal, Ant + Cleo, The Tempest, A Little Touch of Chaos, Much Ado About Nothing, Murder on the Ballarat Train, The Hatpin* and *Kiss Me, Kate*. Kim is currently the Program Leader of the Bachelor of Performing Arts undergraduate degree. She is the winner of the 2015 Vice-

Chancellor's Award for Teaching Excellence, the 2012 EJ Barker Fellowship, a 2010 ALTC Citation, the Yvonne Taylor Award for Directors in 2002 and a joint winner of the 1990 Ewa Czajor Memorial Award. Kim is a Peer Assessor for the Creative Victoria Theatre panel and a founding member of the Australian Women Directors' Alliance. She has a current entry in the Who's Who of Australian Women, and her PhD thesis explores her direction of plays by Caroline playwright Richard Brome, including the Australian premiere of his plays in Ballarat, namely *The City Wit*, *The Antipodes*, *A Jovial Crew*, *Covent Garden Weeded* (re-titled *Garden City Weeded*) and *The Northern Lass*.

ADAM (GUS) POWERS
DESIGNER

Gus is a freelance theatre maker with a Master of Theatre from Monash University who works across both production/stage management and set/costume design roles. Recently as the artistic director of Tasmanian Theatre Company, Gus produced the world premiere of Kate Mulvany's *The Mares* followed by a season of *Gruesome Playground Injuries*, *Constellations* and *Oleanna*. At Federation University's Arts Academy in Ballarat, Gus worked on more than 70 productions between 2008 and 2017 in various roles. Design highlights include: *The Hatpin*; *Urinetown*; *Oklahoma!*; *The Tempest;* and *The Kitchen*. Other productions there include *Oh What A Lovely War*; *Machinal*; *Love and Information*; *As You Like It;* and *Garden City Weeded*. Other freelance work includes: directing / designing Southside Players 2015 production of *Wheeler's Luck* and the 2016 return season at the Theatre Royal in Hobart; designing *The Invisible People* at Sovereign Hill; *Calvin Berger* at the Lawler Studio MTC; Manilla Street's Production of *Blood Brothers* at Chapel Off Chapel; Cheeky Theatre's *Ordinary Days* and *Come Blow Your Horn*; and set and props for Left Bauer/Humdrum Comedy's production of *Gilligan's Island—The Musical* at Chapel Off Chapel. www.adamguspowers.com

JULIE NIHILL
PATRICIA REILLY

Julie is an award-winning Australian theatre, film and television actress with some 35 years' experience. She gained classical training with Trinity College, London, leading to many roles, including Jessie Bradman in the iconic *Bodyline* which firmly established her in the Australian film industry. Julie is widely known as the publican Chris Riley in the multi-award winning *Blue Heelers*.

ELIZABETH SLY
KRYSTAL / RENEE

Elizabeth grew up on the North-West coast of Tasmania and moved to Melbourne to attend La Trobe University, graduating with a Bachelor of Creative Arts (English/Theatre). She has recently completed her Bachelor of Acting for Stage and Screen at the Federation University Arts Academy, where she performed in *The Chapel Perilous* (Mother) directed by Alice Darling, *Our Country's Good* (Elizabeth Morden) directed by Beng Oh, *The Caucasian Chalk Circle* (Governor's Wife) directed by Denny Lawrence, and *The Northern Lass* (Oliver Pate) directed by Kim Durban. Elizabeth is currently undertaking a Master of Teaching (Secondary) at the University of Melbourne. *Running with Emus* is Elizabeth's post-graduate debut on the Melbourne theatre scene.

SAM BAXTER
RAFFAELE / GOOSE

Hailing from the country town of Cohuna, Sam completed his formal training in theatre at Federation University Arts Academy in 2019. Whilst there, he performed in *The Chapel Perilous* (Canon), *Our Country's Good* (Major Ross), *A Woman of No Importance* (Gerald Arbuthnot) and the Australian premiere of *The Northern Lass* (Captain Anvil). This marks Sam's first professional outing as an actor.

KEVIN DEE
JIM / SPARRA

Since his first film role in the hit comedy *Strange Bedfellows*, Kevin has worked on numerous successful short and feature films and won Best Actor Awards in London and the U.S. His theatre work has been well received not only in Australia but also in Canada and at The Edinburgh Fringe. His television work includes *Underbelly*, *Jack Irish*, *Winners & Losers*, *Lowdown* and *Neighbours*.

GREGORY J FRYER
PIE

Gregory has been involved in the arts from 1984 (his last year of school) onwards, initially as a musician then branching out to theatre in 1996. Greg has had a very fulfilling career both in stage and screen. Some of his credits include *The Dr Blake Mysteries*, *The Sapphires* and *Mad as Hell*. However, he considers La Mama Theatre to be his second home and has been an active member of the Lloyd Jones Ensemble for the past 24 years.

STANDING OVATION FOR
AUSTRALIA'S HOME OF INDEPENDENT THEATRE

In 2020 La Mama will celebrate 53 years of nurturing new Australian theatre.

Built in 1883 for Anthony Reuben Ford, a Carlton printer, the building in Faraday Street had been used as a workshop, a boot and shoe factory, an electrical engineering workshop and a silk underwear factory before becoming a theatre in 1967. It was established by Betty Burstall and modelled on experimental theatre activities in New York. Jack Hibberd's play *Three Old Friends* was the first play performed in the tiny space. Since that time the crowded intimacy of La Mama has provided welcome opportunities to a host of playwrights, actors, directors, technicians, film-makers, poets and comedians, such as David Williamson, Barry Dickins, John Romeril, Tes Lyssiotis, Lloyd Jones, the Cantrills, Judith Lucy, Richard Frankland, Julia Zemiro, and Cate Blanchett... the list of those who have been nurtured there is long.

Under the capable care of Liz Jones (Artistic Director and CEO), Caitlin Dullard (Manager/Producer and Co-CEO), and a committed La Mama team, more than 50 productions are produced annually at La Mama, and at a second performance venue, the refurbished La Mama Courthouse, 349 Drummond Street, which was short-listed for a 2018 Victorian Australian Institute of Architects Chapter Award. An ever-increasing audience is drawn not only from the Carlton and Melbourne University environs, but from far and wide across the country.

'I set La Mama up, as a space for writers and directors to perform in but also it was a space where people came, as audience, to participate in the creative experiment.'
—Betty Burstall, Artistic Director of La Mama 1967–76

La Mama Theatre—which on various occasions has been called headquarters, the shopfront and the birthplace of Australian Theatre—was classified by the National Trust in 1999.

'The two-storey brick building is of State cultural significance because it has been occupied by La Mama Theatre… The building is indelibly associated with the performance arts and is a rare manifestation of an experimental theatre in Australia…'
—National Trust Classification Report

Sadly our home in Faraday Street burned down in May 2019. We are in the process of rebuilding and we will reopen there in 2021. Until then, our home is at La Mama Courthouse on Drummond Street Carlton.

La Mama is an open, accessible space, actively breaking down barriers to the Arts through programs, initiatives, affordable ticketing and a welcoming ethos that has developed over the past five decades. La Mama is home to many and open to all.

For bookings and details of all productions and events
visit:
www.lamama.com.au

www.ingramcontent.com/pod-product-compliance
Lightning Source LLC
Chambersburg PA
CBHW050023090426
42734CB00021B/3393